US Army Yearbook 2023

CONTENTS

- 6 The US Army Today
- 10 In The News

Operations
- 14 Reinforcing NATO
- 16 Training Ukraine
- 17 Middle East

Training and Readiness
- 18 NG Trains in Morocco
- 19 Urban Warfare
- 20 Khaan Quest
- 21 Tiger Balm

Kit
- 22 A New Rifle XM5
- 23 XM157 A New Sight for the New Rifle
- 24 Guardian Laser-armed Vehicle
- 25 Augmented Vision System
- 26 High Altitude Balloons
- 27 Electronic Planning Tool

History
- 28 Attack on the Philippines
- 30 Battle of the Bulge
- 32 The Ia Drang Valley
- 34 The Battle of 73 Easting

Organisation And Structure
- 36 Squads to Brigades
- 37 Making a soldier
- 38 Battalions, Task Forces, BCTs
- 39 Divisions
- 40 Order of Battle
- 41 Cyber Warfare
- 42 The US Army around the Globe
- 44 Partnerships around the Globe
- 46 Infantry
- 49 Armour
- 52 Artillery
- 54 Aviation
- 56 Engineers
- 57 Signal Corps
- 58 Combat Support
- 59 Sustainment
- 60 Special Forces
- 63 US Army Reserve
- 64 The National Guard
- 65 National Guard Combat Formations

Equipment
- 66 Acquisition
- 68 M-1 Abrams
- 70 Bradley Fighting Vehicle
- 72 Stryker Armoured Vehicle
- 74 Armoured Cars
- 76 M-109A6 Paladin
- 77 M777 155mm
- 78 M119 105mm
- 79 MLRS/HiMARS
- 81 Air Defence Artillery
- 82 AH-64
- 83 UH-60
- 84 UAVs
- 86 Engineering
- 88 Logistics Vehicles
- 89 Uniforms
- 90 Small Arms
- 92 Communications

Future Army
- 93 Introduction
- 94 Pivot to the Pacific
- 96 USAREUR
- 98 Arctic
- 99 Training with partners
- 100 New Armoured Vehicles
- 102 Autonomous Weapons and Vehicles
- 104 Long Range Artillery
- 106 New Aviation
- 108 Air Defence
- 109 New equipment
- 110 Drones and UAVs

Conclusions
- 112 The Future of the US Army
- 114 Glossary

MAIN COVER IMAGE: US Army soldiers from the 3rd Combined Arms Battalion, 116th Cavalry Regiment and Royal Saudi Land Forces, taking part in Exercise Eager Lion in Jordan, September 11, 2022.
(US ARMY)

LEFT: A US Army M142 High Mobility Artillery Rocket System fires a rocket as part of Nordic Strike 22 at Vidsel Test Range, Sweden, September 27, 2022.
(DOD PHOTO BY ANDERS ÅBERG, SWEDISH MINISTRY OF DEFENSE)

BELOW: US Army Soldiers, assigned to Charlie Battery, 1st Battalion, 134th Field Artillery Regiment, 37th Infantry Brigade Combat Team, fire an M777 Howitzer during an operational rehearsal exercise at Mission Support Site Conoco, Syria, December 4, 2022.
(US ARMY PHOTO BY SGT. JULIO HERNANDEZ)

ISBN 978 1 80282 625 8
Editor: Maj Chris Miskimon ret'd
Senior editor, specials: Roger Mortimer
Email: roger.mortimer@keypublishing.com

Design: PA Media
Cover: Dan Hilliard
Advertising Sales Manager: Brodie Baxter
Email: brodie.baxter@keypublishing.com
Tel: 01780 755131

Advertising Production: Debi McGowan
Email: debi.mcgowan@keypublishing.com

Subscription/Mail Order
Key Publishing Ltd, PO Box 300, Stamford, Lincs, PE9 1NA
Tel: 01780 480404
Subscriptions email: subs@keypublishing.com
Mail Order email: orders@keypublishing.com
Website: www.keypublishing.com/shop

Publishing
Group CEO: Adrian Cox
Publisher: Jonathan Jackson
Head of Marketing: Shaun Binnington

Published by Key Publishing Ltd, PO Box 100, Stamford, Lincs, PE9 1XQ
Tel: 01780 755131
Website: www.keypublishing.com

Printing
Precision Colour Printing Ltd, Haldane, Halesfield 1, Telford, Shropshire. TF7 4QQ

Distribution
Seymour Distribution Ltd, 2 Poultry Avenue, London, EC1A 9PU
Enquiries Line: 02074 294000.

We are unable to guarantee the bonafides of any of our advertisers. Readers are strongly recommended to take their own precautions before parting with any information or item of value, including, but not limited to money, manuscripts, photographs, or personal information in response to any advertisements within this publication.

 © Key Publishing Ltd 2023
All rights reserved. No part of this magazine may be reproduced or transmitted in any form by any means, electronic or mechanical, including photocopying, recording or by any information storage and retrieval system, without prior permission in writing from the copyright owner. Multiple copying of the contents of the magazine without prior written approval is not permitted.

www.keymilitary.com

INTRODUCTION

Welcome

Ongoing responsibilities, constant evolution

ABOVE: A machine gun team of the 1st Cavalry Division provides covering fire for an advancing force during a live fire exercise in Poland. (US ARMY)

Welcome to the very first edition of the US Army Yearbook. On these pages is an in-depth look at the United States Army's current operations, organisation, weapons and equipment, a quartet of history lessons on major battles of its history and a broad look at its preparations for future conflict.

Over nearly two and a half centuries of service, the US Army developed from a collection of militias to a hard-hitting force with worldwide reach. It has suffered its share of defeats and won stunning victories, gradually building a reputation for effectiveness and professionalism. The modern world does not allow the successful to stay perched on their honours, however.

Though still early in its third decade, the 21st century has already seen enormous technological, social, and economic change. The pace of this change will only quicken in the years ahead. As the post-Cold War years give way to a new era of global competition, the threats posed by potential adversaries becomes more diverse. The US Army is feverishly engaged in the effort to determine those threats and develop counters. It is heavily involved in training and equipping the Ukrainian military in its current fight against Russia and is watching closely to draw lessons from the conflict.

The wars in Iraq and Afghanistan have lingering aftereffects, but they are essentially over. While America has no desire to get involved in another counter-insurgency campaign, it must acknowledge the possibility of one arising and be

RIGHT: The 3rd Infantry Regiment (The 'Old Guard') at the Tomb of the Unknown Soldier at Arlington National Cemetery, Virginia. (US ARMY)

ABOVE: A sniper from the Idaho National Guard prepares to fire. (IDAHO NG)

prepared for it. However, the Army must not plan to fight the last war but prepare for the next one. That might mean a major war against a large and capable power, what Army leaders call a 'peer' or 'near-peer' competitor.

What that next conflict will look like is largely uncertain. All the old, familiar weapons are still there – tanks, artillery, helicopters, etc. – but changes are needed in how they are employed in concert with new munitions and sensor systems. Indeed, many of the army's primary weapons systems, such as the M1 Abrams tank, AH64 Apache helicopter and M270 Multiple Launch Rocket System entered service in the 1980s. They have stayed relevant only through frequent upgrades and the addition of digital technology.

These legacy weapons have years or decades of service ahead, but they must be combined with the latest drones, missiles and command and control systems. A tank and its crew might be protected by an autonomous vehicle on its flank. Once the realm of science fiction, energy weapons are becoming practical, and hold promise as an economical way to destroy drone swarms. If an enemy destroys an American satellite its capabilities might be replaced by a high-altitude balloon carrying similar payloads. A unit in need of fire support might receive it from a missile battery 500km away.

All these new weapons must be integrated into a useful and effective force. Testing and exercises are constant, determining how to best use the soldiers and material at hand and forthcoming. These exercises frequently include allied troops from the UK, Australia, Canada, New Zealand, Japan, South Korea and elsewhere.

Allies are as critical as new drones or artillery. The US Army simply cannot operate effectively without them. There are no close physical threats to the American mainland; all its potential adversaries are on the Eurasian landmass. The US Army working alongside allies is a constant theme in this yearbook.

The true power of the US Army are its soldiers. How they are trained, equipped and organised will be shown. The army is in a constant state of evolution, looking forward to the threats of tomorrow, but it still honours its veterans and considers its history.

We hope the US Army Yearbook 2023 informs the reader and sheds light on an army in constant movement around the world as it seeks to deter war while being ready to win one should it start.

Christopher Miskimon
Major, Field Artillery, USA (Ret)
Editor

LEFT: Editor Christopher Miskimon in Slovenia during a NATO exercise, 2014.

THE ARMY TODAY

Eternally in Motion

The US Army in the 21st century

ABOVE: The M2 .50-caliber machine gun, nicknamed the 'Ma Deuce,' has been in service since before World War Two and will remain in use for decades more. (US ARMY)

RIGHT: Gen Mark Milley, Chairman of the Joint Chiefs of Staff, talks to soldiers from the 1st Infantry Division and V Corps in Poland. (US ARMY)

With responsibilities across the globe, in the early 2020s the US Army is in constant motion. Its schedule of exercises, training events and military assistance is so extensive only planners at the top echelons are even aware of everything the Army is doing at any given time. Simultaneously, the need to incorporate new technologies and develop new weapons, equipment, tactics and strategies for the future is daunting, even to senior leaders.

The Ukraine war draws the US Army's focus as well. Though the US is not a combatant in the conflict, it is training large numbers of Ukrainian troops, as it has done since 2014. The bulk of US military aid to Ukraine consists of ground warfare systems, including air defence systems which are used by the US Army. Because of the invasion and the fear of further Russian aggression towards Europe, US Army presence in the region is at its highest level since the 1990s. This is a decided change from the last two decades, when US Army force levels were gradually reduced as American

LEFT: A soldier undergoing Ranger assessment reassembles small arms while undergoing mental stress from his instructors. (US ARMY)

attention concentrated on the Middle East and Indo-Pacific.

The war is also an opportunity for the US Army, though sadly it comes at the suffering of the Ukrainian soldiers and citizens fighting the war. The Army can watch the progress of the war, note the effectiveness of the weapons it has provided, the successes and failures of the soldiers it has trained, and draw valuable lessons for future preparations. This will aid in training not only its own soldiers, but those of partner nations as well. The effects of new technologies are also of prime interest to American planners.

Likewise, the performance of the Russian military is of interest. The mediocre performance of the Russian army thus far is notable, but it is equally notable they are carrying on despite their setbacks. How and where the Russian military improves and how it learns to adapt and use its own technology will inform future US Army planning as well.

Though America is not in a declared war with any state, the US Army is waging a fight on two fronts: current operational responsibilities and preparation for future conflicts. As with any military organisation, this often comes down to budgets. US military spending has vastly increased over the last two decades, reaching $773bn in 2023. The Army is slated for $177.5bn of that figure.

Current operational responsibilities include support to Ukraine, activities in the Middle East, exercises across the Indo-Pacific and training support to dozens of nations across Asia, Central and South America, and Africa. There is a two-fold intent to these operations. First, to assist in creating functional militaries which can stand alone, reducing the need for costly US interventions. Second, to create viable partners so when the US decides it must intervene in a region, it has capable local allies.

Much of this effort has fallen to the National Guard, organised by state, and the federal-level Army Reserve. On average, between 2017 and 2022, about 25,000 Guardsmen and Reservists are activated at any time. Many of them support operations in the Middle East. The State Partnership Program (SPP) »

BELOW: Abrams tanks advance toward the Narew River during the Defender Europe Exercise. This exercise included several NATO allies. (US ARMY)

THE ARMY TODAY

ABOVE: Close combat requires physical skills, showcased in this tournament. Such events build morale and demonstrate soldier's skills. (US ARMY)

BELOW: US and Canadian Paratroopers land on a drop zone in Alaska. (US ARMY)

joins National Guard forces from individual states to allied nations. For example, the Colorado National Guard is partnered with Jordan and Slovenia and provides regular training support to them. This mission helps the National Guard maintain its own readiness through frequent smaller scale deployments.

Preparing for future conflicts is a combination of training, weapons development, and planning. In the battle for budgets, this is one of the US Army's greatest challenges. With US attention shifting toward a heavier involvement in the Indo-Pacific, critics argue the Army must shrink to provide for increases in the Navy and Air Force.

There is some truth to this statement. The Chairman of the Joint Chiefs of Staff, Army Gen Mark Milley, acknowledged the reality of shifting priorities. "Look, I'm an Army guy," he said. "And I love the army... but the fundamental defence of the United States and the ability to project power forward will always be for American naval and air and space power." Rather than a rebuke of the Army, this is a recognition of American's strategic situation and where the army currently fits into it.

Given this acceptance, the US Army is nevertheless preparing to do its part in any conflict the nation may face, including in the Pacific. The new Multi-Domain Task Force (MDTF), discussed later in these pages, is a prime example of an Army effort to prepare for future conflicts. The MDTF's combination of sensor, intelligence, long range artillery fires and air defence blends well with naval and air force's capabilities for a Pacific war. The US Marine Corps is developing similar concepts but lacks the size and depth to do so on the scale needed to fight a major power such as China. This is particularly true if China allies with other powers such as Russia or Iran, creating a two-front war.

Creating such new warfighting organisations has its own difficulties. The US Army's personnel strength is not funded for an increase, and the bulk of the service's support units are in the Reserve and National Guard. With few places to draw soldiers from for new units, the Army may be faced with inactivating combat brigades to source new efforts.

Multi-domain operations – the ability to fight effectively while coordinated in the land, air, sea, space, and cyber realms is key to winning future wars, according to the US Army. The former commander of US Army Pacific, Gen Robert Brown stated this bluntly: "All formations will have to become multi-domain, or they'll be irrelevant."

As part of joint operations, even the Navy recognizes what Army MDTFs contribute. Admiral Harry B. Harris, former commander of US Indo-Pacific Command, said MDTFs will "sink ships, neutralize satellites, shoot down missiles and airplanes, and hack or jam the enemy's ability to command and control."

Digital technology is necessary for new warfighting concepts and the US Army is pushing that into every aspect of its operations. "Going digital is a mindset, it's culture change," said Dr Raj Iyer, the Army's chief information officer. "It's about how we can fundamentally change how we operate as an Army through transformative digital technologies, empowering our workforce, and re-engineering our rigid institutional processes to be more agile." This is an acknowledgement that events occur much more quickly in a digital world, requiring fast responses independent of staff studies and laborious decision-making.

Digitisation also benefits the US Army's legacy systems. Major end items such as the M1 tank and UH60 helicopter entered service decades ago, and upgrades with digital technology have kept them capable. The 2020s may well see the sunset of these older systems, however.

The army has been able to get by with older systems for the last two decades partly because no other nations were developing them either. Now, nations such as China are striving to gain an advantage in military technology, forcing the US to do the same. The US Army has announced six major development initiatives: long range precision fire systems, next generation combat vehicles, future vertical lift (helicopters), air and missile defence, networks, and soldier lethality.

Several of these programmes are already enjoying progress. The army has selected its first truly new infantry rifle since the 1960s. A new transport helicopter has been selected, the Bell V280 Valor. New missile and artillery systems are coming into service in 2023. The true trials will be integrating a mix of new and legacy systems together into a coherent whole which soldiers can use to implement war-winning strategies and tactics.

For the Army of 2023, the stakes have risen from the days of fighting insurgents in the Afghan mountains. Potential adversaries such as China and Russia present much greater, even existential threats to the United States. The true goal of all the training, planning and weapons development is to prevent such a war from occurring. Army leadership understands this. As Gen Milley stated: "There are very few things as expensive as preventing a war. But there are two that are more expensive. One is fighting a war. And the most expensive of all is fighting and losing a war."

ABOVE: Soldiers of the 4th Infantry Division take part in an air assault training mission at Fort Carson Colorado. (US ARMY)

US Army Strength 2022-23		
Component	Brigade Combat Teams	End Strength
Regular Army	31	485,000
National Guard	27	336,000
Army Reserve	0	189,500

IN THE NEWS

Army Expands Arctic Capabilities

Army reactivates 11th Airborne Division for Arctic duty

RIGHT: A veteran of the 11th Airborne places the shoulder patch of his division on the uniform of a newly inducted soldier during the unit's reflagging ceremony, June 6, 2022. (US DOD)

FAR RIGHT: A staff sergeant practices aiming an M18 Claymore mine using a simulator device while participating in the 11th Airborne's Best Squad Competition. (US ARMY)

The Arctic is a new region for conflict between nations, and the US Army is preparing to face the challenges of warfare in the far north. Snow and ice in the northern latitudes continues to melt, exposing ground previously covered, sometimes for millennia. Natural resources and water routes heretofore inaccessible are now becoming the subjects of international debate as to their ownership. Russia has claimed control of many areas above the Arctic circle and appears to be arming itself to fight for them. The United States is now responding with its own military preparations.

To support this effort the army is reactivating an airborne division which cased its colours in 1965. The 11th Airborne Division, originally raised during World War Two, saw combat in the Philippines and sent units to fight in the Korean War. It was later used to test the new technology of helicopters before being deactivated. On May 5, 2022 the Army announced it was reflagging US Army Alaska as the 11th Airborne Division, taking the 12,000 soldiers currently stationed in Alaska and bringing them into a single unit and chain of command. The division formally activated on June 6, 2022.

Two brigades from the Hawaii-based 25th Infantry Division have been transferred to the 11th Airborne. Both were already stationed in Alaska. The 25th's 1st Stryker Brigade Combat Team has become the 1st Brigade, 11th Division while the 4th Brigade 25th Division is now the 11th's 2nd Brigade. The 1st Brigade will turn in its Stryker armoured vehicles and acquire helicopters, becoming something akin to what the US Army calls an air assault brigade. It will also receive specialised ground vehicles tailored for arctic use, which the army is now testing. The 2nd Brigade is an airborne brigade, one of only five in the army and the only one on the country's west coast.

The 1st and 2nd Brigades are stationed at Fort Wainwright and Joint Base Elmendorf-Richardson, respectively. The ceremony marking the conversion of both units to the 11th Airborne was attended by retired veterans of the unit, who placed the 11th's distinctive shoulder patch on their new comrades. Army Chief of Staff Gen James McConville stated, "Experience has told us that units that have a common unit identity is a source of pride. It's extremely important. And the history of a unit and the patch matter."

The 11th Airborne will become the army's specialist unit for arctic warfare. It will improve existing techniques for operations in conditions of extreme cold and high altitude. The division leadership is contemplating how it would serve in locations as varied as Finland and Sweden on NATO's northern flank to the Himalayas in India and Nepal. To that end, US Army leaders have engaged with their Nepalese counterparts to coordinate bilateral training, including the possibility of a joint expedition on Mount Everest. Training events have already occurred in Norway and India.

BELOW: Paratroopers of the 11th Airborne Division make their first parachute drop from a C130 aircraft in Alaska on June 15, 2022. (US ARMY)

US ARMY YEARBOOK 2023

Training Ukrainian Forces

New York National Guard takes over US Training Contingent

The Joint Multinational Training Group – Ukraine (JMTG-U) works to train and professionalise the Ukrainian armed forces. It began operating in Spring 2015 after the 2014 war between Russia and Ukraine resulted in Ukraine's loss of Crimea. Initially the mission took place within Ukrainian borders, largely at the Yavoriv Training Centre 10 kilometres from the Polish frontier. When Russia openly invaded Ukraine in February 2022, this training mission continued, but moved to the Grafenwoehr training area in Germany.

On August 8, 2022, 140 soldiers from the New York National Guard's 27th Brigade Combat Team formally took charge of the JMTG-U at a transfer of authority ceremony, relieving a unit of the Florida National Guard which had filled the role since November 2021. The use of reserve component troops from the National Guard is common in such training missions. This takes advantage of the Guard's combat experience from the War on Terror and helps keep the Guard integrated into the army as a whole force.

LEFT: American soldiers assigned to train Ukrainian forces wear a distinctive advisor's patch to signify their role during a ceremony in Grafenwoehr, Germany. (US ARMY)

The JMTG-U left Ukraine shortly before the war started and has since trained groups of Ukrainian soldiers for the combat they will face when they return home and deploy to the front lines. "We started this mission in Ukraine, completed an unexpected and hasty move to Grafenwoehr, and worked through a lot of change. But one thing has remained constant: our commitment to Ukraine," said Col Jerry Glass, commander of the Florida unit which recently returned home.

At Grafenwoehr, Ukrainians are trained in a variety of military skills, from basic soldiering to the use of the weapons and equipment coming to Ukraine from around the world. This includes the M142 HiMARS rocket system, which has seen extensive use in the current war targeting Russian ammunition depots, headquarters and logistics facilities. A crew can be trained to use the HiMARS effectively in three weeks.

BELOW: A New York National Guardsman walks a line of Ukrainian tanks and BMPs during a battalion field training exercise at Yavoriv, Ukraine. (US ARMY)

www.keymilitary.com

IN THE NEWS

Back to Somalia

US troops return to Somalia and attack al-Shabab

RIGHT: Somali soldiers and first responders evacuate passengers from a crashed airplane at Mogadishu airport on July 18, 2022. US Army soldiers assisted with immediate first aid. (US ARMY)

On May 16, 2022, US President Joe Biden signed an order returning American troops to Somalia to support Somali forces fighting al-Shabab, the Islamist extremist group affiliated with al-Qaeda. About 500 troops redeployed from other missions under US Africa Command (AFRICOM), demonstrating that the United States remains committed to combatting terrorist groups despite the war in Ukraine and increasing tensions with China.

Prior to this redeployment, Army troops did short training missions and operations in Somalia, called 'commuting to work'. However, these periodic visits were considered inefficient and ineffective. A more permanent force allows continuity of action, without significantly increasing AFRICOM's presence in the region.

By mid-July, American troops were engaged in training local forces and by July 17 had already engaged al-Shabab, killing two enemy fighters. The mission took a more humanitarian form when a Jubba Airlines passenger aircraft crash landed at Mogadishu International Airport on July 18. Three American soldiers training Somali Danab Brigade commandos responded with the Somali troops to provide medical assistance to the injured. The trio of US trainers set up a triage station as Danab commandos pulled the survivors from the wreckage. They performed first aid and helped local responders evacuate 16 injured people to local hospitals.

BELOW: Infantrymen from the East Africa Response Force (EARF) debark from a C130 aircraft to provide security at the US Embassy in Mogadishu, Somalia during a readiness exercise. (US DOD)

Veterans Honoured at Bayonet Hill

Celebrating the soldiers who carried out the US Army's last bayonet charge

Each year in February, the US and South Korean militaries commemorate the Battle of Bayonet Hill, fought during the Korean War on February 7, 1951. This battle is notable for the last known bayonet charge conducted by American troops. Members of both armies gather with surviving veterans of the battle for a ceremony which includes a wreath-laying and a rifle salute. These veterans are honoured by American and South Korean soldiers standing next to each other in formation, celebrating the way the two armies fought together seven decades ago.

In early February 1951, Chinese and North Korean soldiers held the high ground on Hill 180, stubbornly defending it against repeated attacks by United Nations troops. Company E, 27th Infantry Regiment, 25th Infantry Division, commanded by Capt Lewis L. Millett, was among the units sent to assault the hill and soon came under heavy fire. His 1st Platoon became pinned down, so Millett brought his 3rd Platoon forward, ordered his men to fix bayonets, and led them in a charge up the hill. Despite the heavy enemy fire, Millett moved ahead of his troops, bayoneted two enemy soldiers, threw hand grenades, and used his rifle as a club.

ABOVE: Capt Lewis Millett leads his troops against Chinese positions on Bayonet Hill. Millett was known for his handlebar moustache and aggressive leadership. (US ARMY)

All the while, he shouted encouragement to his men, as he dodged grenades thrown at him by the enemy and even a few from his own excited soldiers. Eight grenades missed him, but a ninth blasted shrapnel into his legs and back. Despite his wounds, Millett led his men to the top of the hill, where they joined him in driving their opponents back at bayonet point, causing the Chinese and North Koreans to "flee in wild disorder," according to a later citation.

For his courageous act, Millett was presented with the Medal of Honor, the United States' highest award for valour. He received it on July 15, 1951, from then-president Harry S. Truman. Millett had a long career in the US Army, serving in World War Two, Korea, and Vietnam. Before the United States entered World War Two, then-Private Millett left his unit and joined the Canadian army, thinking the US would not enter the conflict. In 1942, while serving in England, Millett turned himself in to the US embassy. The army court-martialled him for desertion, fined him $52, but then commissioned him a few weeks later. Millett served in the army until 1973 and died November 14, 2009.

The ceremony is held at a memorial site at Osan Air Base, a United States Air Force facility which occupies the ground where the battle took place. While there is some argument that the battle in fact occurred on a hill a few miles away, the memorial includes a commemorative plaque and is a fitting tribute to the courage shown by Millett and his soldiers.

LEFT: Korean War veteran Earnest Lee renders a salute with American and South Korean officers during the 71st Hill 180 remembrance ceremony on February 4, 2022. (US DOD)

ARMY HISTORY: BOSNIA

Reinforcing NATO

Re-expanding US Army forces in Europe

RIGHT: An M142 HIMARS launches a rocket during Exercise Nordic Strike in late September 2022. Long-range precision artillery fire has been proven vital to operational successes by the Ukrainian army. NATO commanders have taken note of it. (US DOD)

BELOW: Soldiers from the 101st Airborne Division arrive in Romania in June 2022, to replace paratroopers from the 82nd Airborne. Such rotation of forces increases the number of soldiers with experience operating on NATO's eastern flank. (US ARMY)

The US Army maintained a massive force in Europe during the Cold War. In the 1980s, in Germany alone, the army had two full corps, each with one armoured and one mechanised infantry division, an armoured cavalry brigade and supporting units. After the Soviet Union dissolved in 1991, this force was gradually reduced until by the 2010s there were only four combat brigade-sized elements in Europe, spread through Germany and Italy. This included a cavalry regiment, airborne, artillery and aviation brigades.

In addition to these combat units, the army maintained an extensive theatre support network of logistics and support units. This infrastructure was kept in place to enable army forces to quickly deploy to Europe in the event of a crisis. This decision proved prescient when Russia began to behave more aggressively, including their thinly disguised attack on Ukraine in 2014, which resulted in the Russian seizure of the Crimea.

While Russia did not present the same threat as its predecessor, the Soviet Union, it still posed a danger to its bordering neighbours. Many of these nations had joined NATO, but still lacked the defensive capability to fend off a Russian attack without assistance. The Baltic states of Estonia, Latvia, and Lithuania were particularly vulnerable since the only land route to these three countries could be easily interdicted by the Russians. Additionally, several other NATO nations, perceiving no real threat since the Cold War ended, had allowed their own military capabilities to atrophy.

As a result, US Army combat brigades and task forces are deploying to Europe on a rotational basis. These units serve alongside capable military forces from NATO partners such as the United Kingdom, Canada, and Germany, joining troops from the host nations in which they are stationed.

US ARMY YEARBOOK 2023

ABOVE: A US Army AH64 Apache attack helicopter flies over a Polish Leopard 2 tank during an exercise in Poland in May 2022. (US ARMY)

LEFT: Casualties are inevitable in war. This medical unit is practicing the operation of a field hospital in Germany. (US ARMY)

This effort was substantially increased after Russia invaded the Ukraine in 2022.

A major step was the reactivation of V Corps in February 2020. This headquarters formation can control and coordinate the activities of US Army troops in Europe. V Corps is now permanently stationed in Poland, where it has responsibility for protecting NATO's eastern flank. Since February 2022, the US has sent two BCTs, one infantry and one armoured, an artillery battalion equipped with M142 HIMARS and supporting units to join the existing brigades which now fall under V Corps control. Armoured and Aviation Brigades will rotate through Poland.

Another rotational BCT will be posted in Romania. Smaller task forces serve in the Baltics nations. Germany is now host to an air defence artillery brigade headquarters, an air defence battalion, an engineer brigade headquarters, and a sustainment battalion headquarters. An air defence battery has joined the 173rd Airborne Brigade in Italy. V Corps now has substantial combat power available for Europe's defence. As of June 2022, all these forces are on a heightened readiness status.

Aside from the permanent and rotational forces, V Corps also oversees training exercises with NATO partners and the construction and maintenance of infrastructure such as storage areas and airfields.

The army possesses a large amount of prepositioned equipment which must be maintained in a state of readiness. In the event of war, units from the United States can be flown to Europe in a matter of hours and be issued their weapons and equipment from the prepositioned stocks. These units would be quickly ready for combat operations. The prepositioned equipment concept is a holdover from the Cold War when entire division's worth of equipment sat warehoused and ready for use.

This substantial deployment of force back to Europe is expensive. The US pays for it through the European Defence Initiative, an effort designed not only to fund American units, but to conduct training exercises with host nation forces and provide equipment and weapons to NATO partners on an as-needed basis. Such assistance proved invaluable to the Ukrainians in their current war with Russia and will make NATO forces much more effective if that conflict should spread west.

BELOW: US and Romanian soldiers practice air assault operations. Properly used and protected, helicopters provide mobility and speed to infantry units. (US ARMY)

www.keymilitary.com 15

OPERATIONS

Training the Ukrainian Military

An ongoing effort to support Ukraine's defence against Russian aggression

TOP: A US Army Medic debriefs two Ukrainian medics from the 92nd Mechanized Brigade after a training exercise. (US ARMY)

The US Army's training assistance to Ukraine began in 2014, after the first Russian-led attacks on Ukraine in Crimea and the Donbass regions. This assistance has only accelerated since the open Russian invasion which began in February 2022.

Since January 2021, the US has given billions of dollars in military aid to Ukraine. Along with the contributions of other nations around the world, it has proven vital to Ukrainian soldiers in first defending their territory against invasion, and then retaking it wherever possible.

This assistance includes millions of rounds of ammunition, Javelin anti-tank missiles, Stinger anti-aircraft missiles, drones, cannon and rocket artillery, and counter-battery radar systems, among myriad other items. These systems have augmented and, in many cases, replaced the ageing Soviet-era weapons Ukraine has used since the end of the Cold War.

New weapons bring new capabilities for Ukrainian soldiers, so they must learn how to best employ them and coordinate their effects, such as artillery systems being used to best support infantry and armour and to inflict damage in Russian rear areas. They must also learn to maintain some very modern and effective systems.

This is where in-person training becomes crucial. Tens of thousands of Ukrainian troops have received training from the US Army since 2014. When the 2022 conflict loomed and intelligence estimates pointed toward invasion, the US trainers in Ukraine were withdrawn to locations in Poland and Germany and Ukrainian troops went there for continuing instruction. This prevented US personnel from becoming directly involved in the war and expanding the crisis it created.

Several areas of focus have emerged. US soldiers gave attention to building a strong body of non-commissioned officers, long known to be the backbone of effective western armies. Once combat began, small Ukrainian units led by sergeants proved able to outmanoeuvre and outfight their Russian opponents, who lack professional NCOs. Another area of success is in the use of artillery to support ground forces and disrupt Russian logistics. It is obvious that training support from the US, UK, and other NATO allies have made a drastic difference in the Ukraine War.

RIGHT: Norwegian and American soldiers train Ukrainian artillery soldiers on the 155mm howitzer in May 2022. These weapons were provided as part of security assistance packages from NATO nations. (US ARMY)

FAR RIGHT: A Ukrainian soldier lays down suppressive fire with his PK machine gun during a US-led training exercise in Hohenfels, Germany. (US ARMY)

US ARMY YEARBOOK 2023

The Middle East

Supporting Stability in the Region

Despite the nominal end of combat operations in Iraq and Afghanistan, the US Army maintains an extensive presence throughout the Middle East. Some of those troops, however, still find themselves engaged in fighting, while others are involved in training allied forces. Despite American attention focusing elsewhere, its presence in the region will likely continue for decades.

Although less frequent since the 2019 defeat of the main so-called Islamic State (IS) forces, fighting still takes place in Syria, either against remnants of that group or Iranian-backed militias. US Army forces are a major component of the Combined Joint Task Force – Operation Inherent Resolve, which states its mission as advising, assisting, and enabling local forces until they can independently defeat IS elements in Iraq and Syria.

Many of the forces remaining in Syria are Special Forces soldiers, with support elements to provide security, logistics and fire support. The main US-occupied base in Syria is at Al-Tanf, with up to 200 US soldiers in residence. In late 2022, the base was subjected to a series of attacks including a rocket attack carried out by Iranian-backed militia. Three American troops were wounded. Indirect fire attacks occur frequently in the area, along with occasional drone attacks.

ABOVE: US vehicles operating in Syria typically fly large American flags for identification, to reduce the chances for a friendly fire incident or inadvertent engagement with Russian forces. (US ARMY)

American forces have established deconfliction measures with Russian forces in Syria to prevent inadvertent hostilities between the two nuclear powers. These have been successful; in October 2022, Russian and American patrols passing each other even stopped and exchanged friendly greetings, posed for pictures with each other and exchanged uniform patches. With the Ukraine War souring US-Russian relations, this was a sign the Russians wished to maintain deconfliction.

Aside from lingering active operations, US Army troops engage in noncombat missions with Allied nations including Kuwait, Jordan, Bahrain and elsewhere. These missions are a combination of training exercises and support to local militaries. The US troops carrying out these missions also provide a small but potent force on hand in case of a crisis.

LEFT: Training never stops, even on active operations. American and Norwegian troops practice medical evacuation procedures at Al Asad airbase, Iraq. (US ARMY)

TRAINING AND READINESS

Exercise African Lion

Africa Command's Premier Multinational Exercise

RIGHT: US and Moroccan Special Forces soldiers practice Close-Quarters Battle drills (CQB) in a specially designed 'shoot house' during Exercise African Lion 2022. (US ARMY)

A full range of military capabilities were tested in desert sands of Morocco, Ghana, Senegal, and Tunisia during the month of June 2022. Exercise African Lion is the largest multinational training exercise carried out by US African Command (AFRICOM), the headquarters overseeing Army operations on the African continent. Over 7,500 troops took part in the event. They come from all components of the US military, the four host nations, Brazil, Chad, France, Italy, the Netherlands, and the United Kingdom.

The US Army contingent included active-duty troops from the 1st Cavalry Division, and National Guard troops from Utah, California, Texas, Wisconsin, and Idaho. The Utah National Guard is paired with Morocco under the State Partnership Program, where each state's National Guard works with the military of an allied nation to provide training assistance.

This year's exercise included a joint task force command post event, maritime and air exercises, chemical-biological-radiological-nuclear response training, and a humanitarian assistance event. A joint forcible entry using paratroopers led into a field exercise, culminating in a combined arms live fire exercise using artillery, AH64 attack helicopters, and Special Forces troops.

The Idaho National Guard's 1st Battalion, 148th Field Artillery Regiment deployed with their M109A6 Paladin 155mm self-propelled howitzers for the live fire portion. The battalion's operations officer, Maj Ryan Batt, spoke about the desire to increase tactical proficiency among the participating armies. "Right now, the Moroccans shoot from the M109A5," an older version of the Paladin using manual gunnery techniques instead of the digital systems on the Paladin. "We rely on technology, but it is essential to learn from the Moroccans when it comes to manual operations. There is a time and a place for both operations, and it's beneficial to understand each one."

These exercises also allow National Guard units to exercise shipping their equipment and vehicles overseas, which they would have to do during an actual deployment. After training with their Moroccan and multinational counterparts, the live fire exercise began with AH64 Apache attack helicopters from the Utah National Guard roaming over the simulated battlefield while the Idaho artillery soldiers fired 155mm high-explosive and smoke rounds to support the infantry component.

A new facet of warfare was practised by a US 3rd Special Forces Group cyber warfare team joining Moroccan Special Forces troops to develop prototype cyber effects training. Fighting in the digital realm is part of the 'multi-domain' environment the US Army expects to conduct battle in during future conflicts.

BELOW: An M109A6 Paladin howitzer from the Idaho National Guard's 148th Field Artillery Regiment fires a 155mm high explosive round during a live-fire exercise in Morocco, June 19, 2022. (US ARMY)

The Finnish Summer Exercise

Urban Warfare Training in Northern Europe

Combat in urban areas is one the most intense and dangerous types of operations soldiers face. It requires a high level of skill, discipline, and teamwork which can only be acquired through training. Finnish and American soldiers honed their urban warfare skills in June and July 2022 at Santahamina Island, a few kilometres southeast of Helsinki. The exercise was part of increased defence cooperation between the United States and Finland as the northern European country seeks NATO membership due to the Russo-Ukrainian War.

Hundreds of soldiers from the US Army's 4th Squadron, 10th Cavalry Regiment of the 4th Infantry Division, the 12th Combat Aviation Brigade and the 3rd Brigade Combat Team, 82nd Airborne Division trained with the Guard Jaeger Regiment of the Finnish Army during June and July. This Finnish regiment is responsible for training conscripts and reservists in urban warfare for the defence of Helsinki. Two Jaeger (light infantry) and two Military Police companies are assigned to the regiment along with support units.

American 'sappers', combat engineers specially trained in supporting frontline troops, cooperated with their Finnish counterparts to practise the demolitions work necessary to make forced entry into buildings. This can include placing explosive charges to open doors or make large holes in walls to facilitate movement between buildings during combat. American troops were also trained in how to use Finnish demolitions equipment and the use of field-expedient explosives.

US Army Lt Col Jason Teplesky, commanding the 4th Squadron, 10th Cavalry, explained the importance of the exercise: "It is very important, cooperation between Finnish and American forces. We will continue with these exercises throughout the summer... and move from the group and squad level to the battalion command post exercise, flying our unmanned aerial systems, and we're firing mechanised artillery."

ABOVE: US Army Combat Engineers blast open a window during urban warfare training with the Finnish Guard Jaeger Regiment, June 28, 2022. (US DOD)

LEFT: A Bangalore torpedo detonates during training with US and Finnish troops. Bangalores are used to clear obstacles such as barbed wire and light fortifications. (US DOD)

TRAINING AND READINESS

Khaan Quest

Improving Security for Northeast Asia

RIGHT: A Mongolian officer stands in front of American troops participating in the opening ceremony of the Khaan Quest Exercise, which focuses on peacekeeping skills. (US DOD)

The Five Hills Training Area is the location of the Mongolian Army's Peace Support Operations Training Centre. From June 6-17, 2022, soldiers from 15 nations participated in Khaan Quest 2022, a training exercise co-sponsored by US Indo-Pacific Command and hosted by the Mongolian armed forces. This year's exercise marks the 20th anniversary of Mongolia's first United Nations peacekeeping mission.

Over a thousand personnel took part in the exercise, which focuses on peace-keeping operations, including cooperation with humanitarian organisations and interoperability with host nations during crisis periods. Specific training events included a battalion-level field training exercise and a brigade-level command post exercise designed to give military staff units experience during a realistic peacekeeping scenario. Training tasks from logistics to force protection and even veterinary medicine were practised.

The US Army regularly combines soldiers from both the active and reserve components for such exercises to improve experience across the force and allow different types of units to work together. Khaan Quest 2022 included troops from the regular army's newly activated 11th Airborne Division and the Alaska National Guard. Lt Col Rafael Pacheco of the Alaska Guard recalled working with Mongolian troops in Afghanistan, saying: "In my experience as an Alaska Guardsman, I experienced first-hand Mongolian Armed Forces [MAF] soldiers perform in Kabul, Afghanistan, as part of Operation Enduring Freedom in 2012, Mongolian soldiers performed duties as the force protection contingency in charge of security in Camp Eggers and as flight line security at the Kabul International Airport. MAF Soldiers were amongst the best that ISAF partners could ask for."

Maj Gen Chris Smith, an Australian officer currently serving as deputy commander for US Army Pacific, spoke at the event's closing ceremonies. He stated: "As an Australian officer standing before you speaking on behalf of the United States - as a deputy commander of a force of over 60,000 American troops - I think there are few better illustrations of America's commitment to deep and diverse partnerships."

BELOW: US and UK soldiers meet with Mongolian counterparts during site security training. The exercise focused on protecting a facility distributing food, water, and humanitarian supplies. (US DOD)

US ARMY YEARBOOK 2023

Tiger Balm

US Army Trains with Singapore Armed Forces

ABOVE: American infantrymen lay down suppressive fire with an M240B machine gun during a field exercise. Note the cylindrical blank firing adaptor at the weapon's muzzle. (US ARMY)

In June 2022, the armies of the United States and Singapore conducted a bilateral training exercise designed to foster interoperability between their respective forces. Exercise Tiger Balm 2022 was co-sponsored by US Army Pacific (USARPAC) and the Singapore Armed Forces. The exercises have taken place annually for the past 41 years, the first being held in 1981.

This year's exercise focused on an integrated urban warfare field problem, conducted at the Singaporean army's Murai urban training facility. Soldiers from the US 2nd Infantry Division's 1st Stryker Brigade Combat Team and the Hawaii National Guard's 29th Infantry Brigade Combat Team worked with troops from the 5th Singapore Infantry Regiment to exchange tactics using their respective armoured vehicles. The American units field the Stryker Infantry Carrier Vehicle while Singapore uses the similar Terrex vehicle.

Singaporean Platoon Commander Capt David George described the degree of cooperation between the two armies. "The whole realism of this exercise allows us to understand each other's weaknesses and strengths and cover the gaps."

Leaders of the two armies focused on what they consider the three components of interoperability: human, procedural and technical. The human facet focuses on soldiers working together and understanding each other's tactics and capabilities. Learning each other's procedures allows the two armies to understand how each will plan, act, and react in combat. Technical factors include the interoperability of communications equipment, sharing of logistics resources and munitions, and sharing of information.

As the United States becomes increasingly concerned about the growing military power of China, exercises with partner nations in the region gain new importance. A potential campaign against China would require a network of allies, particularly with nations such as Singapore, which sits astride the shipping lanes China needs to support its economy. It is thus a prospective target for Chinese attack and a possible base for operations.

LEFT: Two battalion commanders, Singaporean Lt Col Abu Bakar and American Lt Col Jacob Cross, pose for a picture during a field training exercise in Tiger Balm 2022. (US ARMY)

THE LATEST KIT

A New Rifle: The XM5

The Army's first new standard rifle in over 50 years

RIGHT: The new XM5 rifle gives infantry soldiers increased firepower, particularly against opponents wearing modern body armour. It is based on an existing, proven design. (US ARMY)

In 2022 the army made a historic decision to replace the long-serving M16/M4 series of rifles with a new weapon, the XM5. This rifle is a new design to be manufactured by SIG-Sauer, a German company with production facilities in the United States. The XM5 is a development of SIG's MX rifle currently in production, which externally resembles the M4 but uses a short-stroke piston system, producing less carbon build-up in the weapon during heavy usage, and increasing reliability.

Normally a major weapons system procurement takes years or decades of testing but the XM5 went from the initial competition to selection in just 27 months. The rifle is based on existing designs and so is evolutionary rather than revolutionary; this sped up the development process considerably. The Army sought the new rifle and a companion light machine gun through the Next Generation Squad Weapon Program (NGSW), awarding the contract to SIG-Sauer in April 2022.

Weighing 3.8kg (8.4lb), the XM5 fires an innovative new 6.8x51mm cartridge, designed to give improved penetration through body armour, which is becoming increasingly present on modern battlefields. Since the round is heavier, it also has increased effective range compared to the lightweight 5.56mm bullets in current use since the 1960s. This new ammunition will replace the current 5.56x45mm NATO round. The new rifle's magazine will hold 20 rounds of 6.8mm ammunition with a soldier's basic load comprising seven magazines for 140 rounds total. It can also be fitted with a sound suppressor

The weapon is expected to enter service in the last quarter of 2023. Priority of issue will go to soldier's expected to engage in close combat, such as infantrymen, cavalry scouts, combat engineers, medics, and artillery forward observers.

BELOW: Over 100 distinct technical tests validated the weapon's improved reliability and effectiveness over the current M4 carbine, giving soldiers an edge on future battlefields. (SIG SAUER)

US ARMY YEARBOOK 2023

XM157 Squad Weapon Optic

An Advanced Sight for the Infantry

LEFT: The XM157 will replace the current range of optical sights and laser projectors, such as those on this M4 carbine, saving weight and reducing the number of batteries a soldier needs to carry. (US ARMY)

BELOW: The XM157 combines the features of a number of devices into one system mounted on the soldier's primary weapon, simplifying their ability to engage targets quickly. (US ARMY)

The Army has selected a new rifle to replace the venerable M16/M4 series and a new light machine gun to replace the M249 Squad Automatic Weapon (SAW). Modern infantry weapons require optical sighting systems for the soldier to utilise their full potential. The new weapons fire a larger cartridge than the weapons they're replacing with longer effective range and better penetration against modern body armour. To answer this requirement, a new sighting system is being developed.

The XM157 is the product of the Next Generation Squad Weapon – Fire Control program. Produced by Vortex Optics of Wisconsin, USA, the contract calls for up to 250,000 XM157s to be delivered over a 10-year period. Production was due to begin in late 2022.

The new sight combines several useful instruments in a single integrated unit. The most basic feature is a 1-8x30 Low-Powered Variable Optic (LPVO) with a glass-etched reticle lens. The XM157 also has both a laser rangefinder and

aiming laser along with a ballistic computer to aid accuracy. An environmental sensor measures conditions that affect the bullet's trajectory and adjusts the soldier's aiming point. The firing solution is computed in tenths of a second. A digital compass and wireless communications help the soldier to know their location and stay connected on the modern battlefield. A display can be projected onto the optic's first focal plane to account for bullet drop over distance, show navigational waypoints, highlight identified threats, and show fields of fire.

Such a device has to be tough to withstand the rigours of field use. The XM157's testing included extreme heat and cold, immersion testing, drop testing and live fire trials using tens of thousands of rounds of ammunition. It is controlled using a keypad or by a detachable remote. This new sighting system is a jump forward in precision and versatility for infantry small arms.

www.keymilitary.com

THE LATEST KIT

Energy Weapons for Air Defence

Lasers weapons are viable against drones and manned aircraft, even artillery shells

RIGHT: Two soldiers examine a drone shot down by a Guardian vehicle during testing at Fort Sill, Oklahoma. The weapon has shown increasing ability to engage multiple targets quickly. (US ARMY)

The proliferation of drones and other unmanned aerial systems (UAS) is a fast-growing threat to ground forces. They join the already substantial threat from fixed- and rotary-wing aircraft and munitions including rockets, missiles, artillery shells and mortar bombs. On a fast paced 21st century battlefield, these systems can combine to overwhelm existing defences.

The US Army's answer to this problem is the Manoeuvre – Short Range Air Defence (M-SHORAD), a Stryker armoured vehicle mounting the Multi-Mission High Energy Laser (MMHEL). This eight-wheeled infantry carrier is converted to carry a 50-kilowatt (kW) laser. The laser is capable of defeating UAS and some rocket, artillery, and mortar rounds. The army has named this vehicle the Guardian.

M-SHORAD resulted from a competition under Kord Technologies, who serve as prime contractor on the effort. Subcontracts were awarded to Northrop Grumman and Raytheon.

BELOW: A Guardian laser vehicle during testing at White Sands Missile Range in March 2022. The vehicle is equipped to power multiple shots of its 50kW laser. (US ARMY)

The Northrop system encountered difficulties, so the Army moved forward with the Raytheon design. Raytheon received a $123 million contract to produce the prototypes, though the army may reopen the competition since such air defences are critical to future operations. A 100kW system is envisioned to improve capabilities.

A four-vehicle battery of Guardians was delivered in 2022 for further testing. This research will focus on protecting a brigade combat team from UAS, helicopters, and rockets. The army also wants to study the effectiveness of the 50kW laser against fixed wing aircraft. Previous testing at the White Sands Missile Range in New Mexico proved the basic viability of the system, which must now show durability under field conditions. The Guardian's large-aperture optical system, used for the laser, can also provide long range observation for Intelligence, Surveillance and Reconnaissance (ISR).

The Guardian's ability to shoot down UAS and engage multiple targets shows great promise for air defence on the battlefield. Further, it is doing so at an economical rate, with the average cost per kill only $30. As cheap drones flood the skies over future battlefields, the ability to down them without expending expensive missiles is vital.

Integrated Visual Augmentation System

Next generation mixed reality headset for the soldier

The stresses of the modern battlefield take a toll on soldier's abilities to react quickly, detect and engage targets and make timely decisions. In the Information Age, getting useful data to soldiers is critical. The new Integrated Visual Augmentation System (IVAS) overlays information onto a screen within a pair of goggles the soldier wears. The system provides night vision and thermal sensors, mapping and navigation functions, facial recognition, language translation and target location. The goggles can even link to other sensors, allowing soldiers to see outside of their vehicle or through a distant sensor platform.

As with any new technology, there are deficiencies to be fixed. The programme was intentionally postponed for several months in late 2021 to address issues with display, quality, reliability and to improve battery management. Despite these issues, IVAS has been field tested by soldiers.

The 3rd Battalion, 75th Ranger Regiment tested IVAS in early 2022. Sergeant 1st Class Brian Hayman, a Ranger platoon sergeant, described how the system eliminates human error during land navigation and allows soldiers to move without having to check maps or even use a compass. "You never have to stop and do a map check," he said. "With just the push of a button, you have an arrow that's in the bottom of your screen and you walk the arrow to your point, so there's no accidentally drifting left or right." The Rangers also appreciated the ability to locate fellow soldiers on the battlefield using the system's map function.

Paratroopers of the 82nd Airborne Division tested IVAS in field conditions in late 2022. They trained using various combat scenarios: participating units had to plan, rehearse, and execute nine different missions using IVAS. Unlike normal training events, these exercises were not graded, allowing the soldiers to focus on testing their IVAS goggles and determining how they can be used in combat situations. IVAS has also been tested with aircrews and mechanised infantry.

LEFT: IVAS has also been tested under arctic conditions in Alaska. (US ARMY)

LEFT: A machine gun crew uses their IVAS goggles to scan for targets during a field trial. Target identification is another function of the technology. (US ARMY)

THE LATEST KIT

High Altitude Balloons

Balloons offer target detection and surveillance capabilities

The battlefields of the 21st century are a place where powerful weapons systems remain hidden until needed, emerge to fire, and then quickly retreat to cover or concealment to avoid a fast counter strike. Rocket, missile, and artillery systems are increasingly long ranged, expanding the amount of territory that must be searched and monitored for them. Concern likewise exists about the abilities of widely separated units to communicate, receive orders, or coordinate actions. Long range jamming and sensing systems have likewise proliferated. This has eroded the US Army's long-held advantage in communication, navigation and targeting.

One answer to these challenges is sought in the high-altitude balloons the Army is now testing. For decades, the Army's communications and electronic warfare activities have occurred via satellite or aircraft. These methods worked well because no opponent had anti-satellite or advanced air defence capabilities. However, as the Army prepares to fight peer and near-peer adversaries, the vulnerabilities of space and traditional air assets is of great concern.

Satellites are increasingly vulnerable to destruction and take time to replace. Aircraft are similarly at risk along with their highly trained aircrews. High altitude balloons are unmanned and can carry payloads for electronic warfare, surveillance, jamming and observation. They are more easily replaced when lost and cost less than comparable systems. Theatre commanders can blanket the combat area with these balloons so that they overlap, increasing resiliency.

Development of these balloons was previously held at the Department of Defense level but has now been released to the individual services. Lt Gen Daniel Karbler of the US Army's Space and Missile Defence Command stated: "It's just phenomenal what we're able to do with high-altitude balloons...pennies on the dollar with respect to doing it." He added: "Its tactically responsive support to the warfighter."

In 2021, the army conducted a test of the balloon system in Norway. Operating between 60,000 and 72,000 feet above sea level, the system provided targeting data for an artillery rocket system launch. At such altitudes the balloon provides a useful over the horizon search capability and the balloons are reportedly able to fly as high as 90,000 feet, using wind currents to enter their target area. At least one design uses solar panels to charge its batteries. Other tests have taken place in the Pacific.

BELOW: Soldiers prepare a Thunderhead balloon system for launch during an exercise in the Philippines in April 2022. (US ARMY)

BELOW: GPS-guided rockets launched using targeting data provided by a high-altitude balloon in Norway. (US ARMY)

Electronic Warfare Planning and Management

Controlling a new facet of warfare

During the two decades of war in Afghanistan and Iraq, the US Army's skills at electronic warfare versus a peer or near-peer adversary atrophied. The insurgencies in the Middle East lacked the resources to jam or conduct electronic attacks against Coalition forces, so efforts focused on other priorities. During the 2014 Russian incursion into the Crimea, the Russian military conducted several successful electronic warfare (EW) operations against the Ukrainians. These demonstrations became a warning to rekindle the Army's nascent EW capabilities.

The digital realm has become increasingly important to modern warfare, requiring military units to plan for EW in concert with more conventional forces such as artillery, aviation, and intelligence. To oversee this synergy between EW and the soldier on the ground, the US Army is adopting the Electronic Warfare Planning and Management Tool (EWPMT). It can support US Army units ranging from battalions to joint task forces overseeing multiple brigades and other branches of service, including allied partners. The Army has lacked this capability before now.

The system enables Electronic Warfare Officers (EWOs) to coordinate surveillance, targeting and attack using EW resources, assist with intelligence gathering and manage use of the electronic spectrum. Success allows manoeuvring forces to operate without suffering the effects of enemy jamming, spoofing, or communications eavesdropping. Current development has the system in testing by users to gain feedback on its real-world utility. Chief Warrant Officer Will Flanagan, a senior EW targeting officer at the National Training Centre in Fort Irwin, California, gives EWPMT good marks so far. "I can show the commander where we're at, and what we can do," he reported. "This is the first tool to allow us to do our jobs."

ABOVE: EWPMT allows electronic warfare specialists to oversee digital and cyber effects during combat operations. (US ARMY)

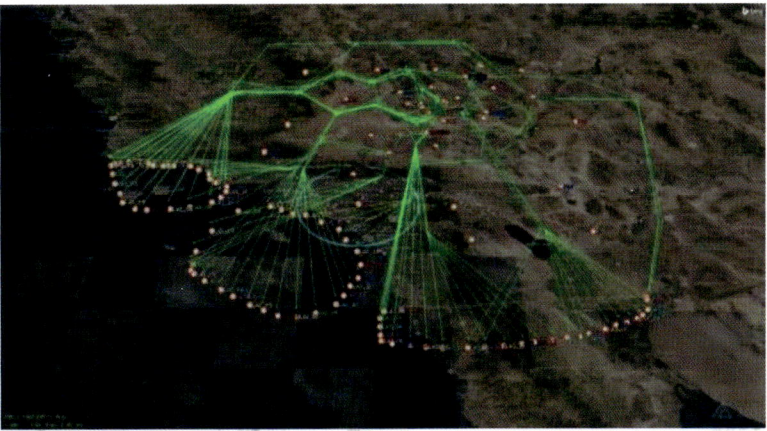

LEFT: The main screens of the EWPMT allow user to visualise the effects of electronic warfare actions and adjust plans for maximum impact. (US ARMY)

HISTORY

Attack on the Philippines

The US Army's brutal introduction to the Pacific War

RIGHT: General Douglas MacArthur led the defence of the Philippines until ordered to evacuate in March 1942. He remains a controversial figure even 80 years later. (US NATIONAL ARCHIVES)

The fires still burned at Pearl Harbor when air forces of the Japanese Empire attacked the US Army Forces Far East (USAFFE), based in the Philippines, on December 8, 1941 (local time). The attack proved a complete success, destroying half the American's aircraft on the ground. The same day a small force from the Japanese 14th Army landed on an island north of Luzon, the first of nearly 130,000 troops they would commit to the conquest of the Philippines. Two days later more troops landed on Luzon itself.

The Japanese planned to capture the Philippines, Malaya, Hong Kong, and the Dutch East Indies in a fast series of campaigns, before their enemies could muster the strength to stop them. Once Japan controlled Southeast Asia with its vast natural resources, its leaders believed they could hold against any counter attacks until the Anglo-American Allies grew weary and sued for peace.

The American plan to hold the islands involved the US Philippine Division, about 10,500 troops, many of them members of the Philippine Scouts, local troops led by mostly American officers. The Philippine Army contributed two regular and ten reserve divisions in varying states of training and readiness. This force fell under the command of Major General Douglas MacArthur, a World War One veteran who held the rank of field marshal in the Philippine army. Just before the war, MacArthur received 8,500 Army Air Force troops along with two tank battalions and an anti-aircraft regiment from the National Guard, giving him about 130,000 troops all told.

In the days following December 8, more Japanese troops landed at different points around Luzon, proving difficult for the meagre American forces to engage decisively. The official plan for the defence of the Philippines, approved and ordered by the US War Department, was to delay any Japanese landings while the army withdrew onto the Bataan Peninsula, a defensible area on the west side of Manila Bay. MacArthur did not engage this plan soon enough, causing needless losses and failing to stock adequate food and supplies on Bataan. Meanwhile, Japanese forces pushed forward relentlessly, ultimately pinning 80,000 troops on Bataan.

Once the Japanese realised the Americans planned to occupy Bataan, they pressed their attacks, hoping to prevent the entire American force from taking refuge there. However, the US tank battalions, and Filipino troops managed to withdraw in good order, inflicting heavy casualties and destroying bridges behind them to slow the Japanese. A series of defensive lines halted Japanese attacks during January through March 1942, but the steadily weakening US force could not counterattack.

The Japanese attempted an amphibious landing behind the American lines on January 23 in coordination with a general attack along those front lines, but the landing was disrupted by a daring attack from a US PT boat. Ashore, ad hoc groups of Air Corps personnel fighting as infantry, landed sailors

RIGHT: Japanese soldiers attempt to breach barbed wire under artillery fire on Bataan. (US NAVY)

BELOW: Its cannon jammed; a US M3 Stuart tank overruns a Japanese roadblock on the Bataan Peninsula in late December 1942. (NATIONAL GUARD)

LEFT: Most of the Allied soldiers who fought in the campaign were Filipinos. These Filipino Scouts have just finished defeating a Japanese landing party. (US NAVY)

and Filipino police forced those Japanese who did land into a small pocket, where they were destroyed by February 13.

With the fighting becoming more desperate and with no ability to relieve or reinforce MacArthur's command, US President Franklin Roosevelt ordered MacArthur to leave the Philippines and go to Australia, which he did in March. Once there, MacArthur made his famous speech proclaiming "I shall return." Meanwhile, his soldiers continued to struggle and die on Bataan.

Despite their losses, the Japanese reorganised and attacked again at the end of March, now facing an American force plagued by hunger, disease, and exhaustion. Most of the US force was overrun, with a few hundred reaching the bastion at Corregidor, a fortified island at the entrance to Manila Bay. Japanese artillery and bombers bombarded Corregidor with high explosives during early May, until Japanese infantry landed on the night of May 5-6.

With the situation now hopeless, the American commander, General Jonathan Wainwright, asked for surrender terms. Around 10,000 men went into captivity from Corregidor, joining tens of thousands more captured earlier. Some troops ignored the surrender order and fled into the jungles to fight as guerrillas. The prisoners suffered years of brutality under the Japanese.

The US force managed to hold out against the Japanese for nearly five months, far longer than expected, but the outcome was never really in doubt, given the impossibility of relief. The Philippines would be liberated in 1944-45.

LEFT: Japanese soldiers celebrate the fall of Bataan. Despite their victory, the five-month campaign proved difficult and costly. (US NAVY)

BELOW: American and Filipino soldiers surrender to Japanese forces on Corregidor Island in May 1942. (US NATIONAL ARCHIVES)

HISTORY

The Battle of the Bulge

The largest battle in US Army history

RIGHT: The first tank to break through the German siege lines at Bastogne bore the name Cobra King. Soon after the Germans were in full retreat. (US ARMY)

The Ardennes is a heavily wooded, hilly region near the German-Belgian border. In December 1944, it was considered a quiet sector, with a poor road network that made large military operations difficult. The Allied command sent new units there to give them a taste of frontline operations before moving them on to more active sections of the front and exhausted units went there to rest and refit. Despite the poor roads and defensible terrain, on December 16, 1944, three German armies with 25 divisions broke through on a 60-mile front, overrunning the six American divisions in their path.

The operation, named Wacht Am Rhein (Watch on the Rhine), was a desperate move by Hitler to divide the Western Allies by driving a wedge of German troops between the Commonwealth forces to the north and American field armies to the south. The plan went forward despite the reservations of many German senior generals. It achieved initial success, surprising the Allied high command, who thought it was a local attack. The German 6th Panzer Army, led by SS General Josep Dietrich, drove forward as the main attack, supported by Gen Hasso von Manteuffel's 5th Panzer Army to his south and Gen Eric Brandenburger's 7th Army screening the entire German left flank. Their advance made a bulge in the US lines on American maps, causing news reporters to give the Ardennes offensive its famous moniker, the Battle of the Bulge.

Even among these early accomplishments, the seeds of German defeat were already sprouting. While many American troops and even whole units collapsed and fled in disarray, others held fast. These small American groups defended vital road junctions and towns, slowing the German advance, and creating time for American reserves to be committed. British troops to the north took up positions to contain the German offensive. The Germans had limited

ABOVE: Soldiers of the 1st Infantry Division push their 57mm anti-tank gun into position on December 17, 1944. The 57mm M1 was a license-built version of the British six-pdr. (US ARMY)

RIGHT: The 'Long Tom' M1 155mm cannon had a range of 23.7km (14.7m). It was used with deadly effect against German positions around Bastogne. (US ARMY)

fuel supplies and each delay emptied the petrol tanks of their vehicles.

In the north, fighting centred around the Elsenborn Ridge, where the defending Americans, untested men of the 99th Division, blunted the German advance, inflicting heavy casualties and fatally upsetting the German timetable. US commanders desperately pressed clerks and cooks into the line as infantry, called in artillery on their own positions and held despite several German penetrations of their lines.

In the centre, the Germans advanced farther but still encountered delays. At the crossroads town of St. Vith, elements of four US divisions held up the German advance for eight days, until December 23, another fatal delay for the German schedule. A few units of the 5th Panzer Army got within sight of their goal, the Meuse River, before a British armoured force ambushed the leading German units, forcing them back.

In the south, the German advance met similar difficulties to those on the northern axis of advance. The experienced US 28th Division, exhausted from recent fighting in the Hurtgen Forest, nevertheless offered stiff resistance despite being so thinly spread the Germans often bypassed them. While their stubborn defence delayed the Germans for only a few days, it was enough for US General Dwight Eisenhower to move his reserves to block further enemy advances. By the time the Germans reached another vital crossroads town, Bastogne, the US 101st Airborne Division was there, supported by a separate artillery battalion and one combat command (equal to a regiment) of the 10th Armored Division.

LEFT: A team of combat engineers in the forest outside Bastogne, Belgium. The front two soldiers each carry a rifle and a bazooka anti-tank rocket launcher. (US ARMY)

BELOW: The skies were clear on December 26, 1944 and hundreds of C47 cargo planes dropped supplies on the garrison at Bastogne. (US ARMY)

The American perimeter held through numerous German attacks. When the German commander demanded the Americans surrender, Gen Anthony McAuliffe, commanding the 101st, replied simply "Nuts!" McAuliffe rarely used profanity and commonly used this term, which was explained to the Germans as 'go to hell'. The 101st held Bastogne until relieved by the 4th Armored Division on December 26. The 4th was one of General George Patton's units. Patton managed to quickly turn part of his 3rd Army north after the battle started, slamming into the German flank, and lifting the siege of Bastogne.

Afterward, American counterattacks gradually pushed the Germans back to their starting points by early February. The loss of Germany's last major armoured reserves weakened them elsewhere, particularly on the Eastern Front. The Bulge is the largest land battle ever fought by American troops, some 700,000 of whom took part in the fighting. About 89,500 were killed, wounded, or captured. The battle is a testament to the endurance and determination of the American soldier under harsh conditions.

HISTORY

The Ia Drang Valley

America's introduction to the Vietnam Conflict

RIGHT: Capt Joel Sugdunis commanded A Company, 2/7 Cavalry, sent to reinforce 1/7 Cavalry at LZ X-Ray. He is conferring with Lt Col Moore. (US ARMY)

The communist insurgency in Vietnam was decades old by the time the United States dedicated ground troops in large numbers. Prior to 1965, most of the American military personnel in Vietnam were advisors and training cadre. When the first American combat troops arrived in 1965, the main threat to South Vietnam lay in the Central Highlands. This heavily forested, mountainous area played host to thousands of North Vietnamese Army (NVA) troops who infiltrated the region and had almost complete freedom of movement.

The activities of these NVA units proved effective enough to draw the attention of the newly arrived 1st Cavalry Division, the US Army's first airmobile division, using helicopters as their primary transport. Helicopters allowed infantry to move quickly around the battlefield to perform searches, establish blocking positions and strike from unexpected directions. The division planned a search operation near a small mountain named the Chu Pong Massif for November 14, 1965.

The unit selected for the mission was the 1st Battalion, 7th Cavalry (1/7), commanded by Lt Col Harold Moore, a veteran of the Korean War. Most of the 440 men in his battalion were new soldiers, well-trained but inexperienced. Their landing zone (LZ) bore the name X-Ray. An open field 200 yards long and 100 yards wide, it could accommodate eight helicopters at a time. It would take six trips to get the entire battalion there.

The first lift took off at 10:35 for the 13-minute flight. Artillery struck the area around LZ X-Ray to suppress any enemy troops. Moore could not know it, but his battalion was about to land near two NVA regiments. He set down at the LZ with B Company. While they awaited the next lift, patrols went out to search for nearby enemy troops. They caught a prisoner who told them of the heavy enemy force nearby. As more American soldiers arrived, they began to push out from the LZ.

At 12:15 rifle fire broke out. B Company ran into an advancing NVA

ABOVE: Air cavalrymen disembark from a UH1 helicopter; such aircraft provided unprecedented mobility to American troops but were vulnerable to ground fire. (US ARMY)

RIGHT: Air support from aircraft such as this A1E Skyraider inflicted terrible casualties on the attacking North Vietnamese Army. (USAF)

LEFT: Helicopters proved vital to resupplying the American troops engaged in the Ia Drang while supporting artillery was equally important in keeping the enemy at bay. (US ARMY)

LEFT: Lt Col Harold Moore commanded the 1st Battalion, 7th Cavalry in the Ia Drang. His leadership proved vital to the unit's hard-won victory. (US ARMY)

force and was soon heavily engaged. Its 2nd Platoon chased a small group of NVA and became cut off. A and C companies linked with B Company to form a perimeter around the LZ. As D Company arrived it was also fed into the perimeter.

At 14:30 a heavy attack struck A and D companies, but two M-60 machine gun teams poured such a heavy fire into the NVA that the attack broke up before it could drive a wedge into the American perimeter, which was fully formed by 15:30. Several attempts to recover the isolated platoon failed. One attack was held up by an NVA machine gun emplaced near a termite mound. Lt Joe Marm fired an anti-tank rocket at it, followed by a grenade, but the enemy weapon remained in action. He charged the termite mound, threw another grenade, and killed the survivors with his rifle. For this action Marm was later awarded a Medal of Honor.

After nightfall, the NVA continued probing the US positions with little success. American artillery kept the enemy at bay, with 4,000 rounds fired the first day and night. The next morning another heavy attacked fell on the Americans, penetrating the perimeter, and again two machine gun crews kept their comrades from being overrun. The rest of the day saw more NVA attacks, beaten back by air strikes, artillery, rifle and machine gun fire. Some reinforcements from other battalions of the 7th Cavalry arrived but they could do little more than replace casualties. Other units also made their way toward LZ X-Ray on foot. A patrol reached the trapped platoon and returned them to the perimeter.

On the third day, the NVA attacked at 04:00, setting off trip flares put out by the US cavalrymen. Small arms fire decimated the NVA and skilled artillery direction by a US forward observer pummelled the NVA with shrapnel and high explosives. At dawn, Moore suspected the enemy was gathering outside his positions and ordered a 'mad minute'. This meant every soldier in the perimeter fired their weapon on full automatic. The firing spooked about 50 enemy troops, who fired back but were quickly killed or driven off.

The battle now ended, the Americans swept the area for the bodies of their dead and 1/7 received orders to withdraw. They lost 79 killed and 121 wounded; NVA losses are unknown, but 634 bodies were counted around LZ X-Ray. The NVA troops had shown bravery and discipline, but American courage, tactics and firepower won the battle. Both sides had shown their strength at the beginning of a long and costly new phase of the Vietnam conflict.

HISTORY

The Battle of 73 Easting

The US Army's last large armour engagement

RIGHT: A US Army doctor treats a wounded Iraqi soldier. (US ARMY)

ABOVE: The Armour Piercing Fin Stabilised Discarding Sabot (APFSDS) ammunition of the M1 Abrams easily penetrated Iraqi tank armour even at long range. (US ARMY)

BELOW: A pair of Abrams and a Bradley IFV move past a coalition convoy in Kuwait. The Abram's turbine engine guzzled fuel but provided high cross-country speed. (US ARMY)

On August 2, 1990, the Iraqi army invaded the small, oil-rich nation of Kuwait. While this attack took the world by surprise, a coalition quickly formed to force Iraq to withdraw if negotiation failed. Iraq's leader, Saddam Hussein, refused to succumb to international pressure, leading to a massive military build-up along the border between Saudi Arabia and Kuwait. The ensuing air campaign caused such damage to Iraqi forces that the war's outcome was essentially decided, but a ground campaign was needed to physically push the Iraqis out.

The ground phase of the Gulf War began on February 24, 1991, with coalition forces quickly piercing the weakened Iraqi lines. Mass surrenders were common and allied troops soon had difficulty containing all their prisoners. One wild card were the 80,000 troops of the Republican Guard, Saddam's best trained and equipped units.

US VII Corps advanced into the Iraqi desert west of Kuwait, screened by the US 2nd Armored Cavalry Regiment (2ACR). The corps was to move north and then pivot right to smash into the Iraqi right flank, a move which would also cut off enemy forces in Kuwait. For the first two days of the advance, little enemy contact was made. US commander Gen Norman Schwarzkopf pressured the VII Corps commander, Gen Frederick Franks, to move faster.

Franks ordered 2ACR forward; the order read: "2ACR attacks east to fix Tawakalna Mechanized Division; on order, 1ID [US 1st Infantry Division] passes through 2ACR to continue the attack east." Each of the regiment's squadrons (battalion sized units in the US Army) covered a zone six miles wide and up to ten miles deep. Their eventual goal was a north-south gridline on their maps referred to as the 73 Easting.

The lead unit in the advance was Eagle Troop, with nine tanks and 13

34 US ARMY YEARBOOK 2023

Bradley IFVs. As they advanced over a small rise, the Americans spotted a line of dug-in T72 tanks. Eagle Troop's commander, Captain H.R. McMaster, ordered a round fired at the nearest T72. Seconds later, another Abrams crew slammed a sabot round into a second T72, sending its turret into the air in a large explosion. More of Eagle Troop's tanks joined the fight, moving at 25mph and firing on the move. Within three minutes 15 enemy tanks had been destroyed.

Behind the Iraqi tanks were dug-in infantry, who opened fire. The American scouts flanked them, raking their positions with cannon and machine gun fire. Some of the fighting became so close that US Bradley commanders were throwing grenades from the hatches of their turrets. Using their thermal sights, the American tankers next spotted 17 more T72s parked in a reserve position, their crews still trying to climb aboard. From a range of 2,000 metres, the Americans opened fire, destroying them all.

Nearby, tanks from Ghost Troop moved through a smoke screen straight into an enemy position filled with tanks and BMPs. As they destroyed the vehicles, Iraqi infantry swarmed from nearby bunkers and attacked the tanks with rocket propelled grenades (RPGs). The Americans pulled back a few hundred yards and smashed the enemy attack with machine gun fire.

As night fell, the Americans chose to setup a defence line two miles ahead of the rest of the regiment. For three hours the Republican Guard counterattacked, hitting Ghost troop hardest. A supporting artillery battery fired 1,100 rounds, smashing the Iraqi forces, and destroying their rear guard. For the loss of a single Bradley, one man killed and six wounded, an entire Republican Guard brigade lay destroyed. The survivors soon surrendered; the Iraqi commander, now a prisoner, told his captors he had lost only two tanks to air strikes but 70 to 2ACR in the first minutes of the American attack.

The victory at 73 Easting was a testament to the rebirth of the US Army after the Vietnam conflict. New weapons and advanced technology played their part, but every field commander praised the training, discipline, and initiative of their soldiers as the factor that won the war. Many American soldiers credited their thorough training by stating the actual war was almost like an exercise. The Battle of 73 Easting was the US Army's most recent large-scale tank battle and has been studied closely ever since.

ABOVE: A Soviet-made T72 MBT lies wrecked in the Kuwaiti desert. Iraq's eastern bloc tanks proved no match for the US Abram's firepower. (US ARMY)

BELOW: 73 Easting is still commemorated by the 2nd Cavalry. A veteran of the battle christens a monument with a captured T-72 for the 25th anniversary in 2016. (US ARMY)

LEFT: A wrecked BMP1 IFV is missing its turret. The intense fighting at 73 Easting left the battlefield strewn with destroyed armour. (US ARMY)

ORGANISATION

How the US Army is Organised

The Building Blocks for a Combat-Ready Force

RIGHT: The crew of an artillery rocket launcher includes a gunner, driver, and commander. Their daily duties revolve around maintaining and employing this weapon system. (US ARMY)

The US Army organises its combat arms units into Brigade Combat Teams (BCTs). These formations are composed of subordinate units of infantry, armour, artillery, and other supporting branches, depending on the BCT's designation as armoured, infantry, airborne (parachute) or air assault (helicopter). The BCT concept has been in use in the US Army since the mid-2000s and is a recreation of the regimental combat teams and armoured combat commands used during World War Two. BCTs provide a flexible combined arms unit which can be tailored to the mission at hand.

The basic building block of the army is the team, usually three enlisted soldiers led by a junior non-commissioned officer. Two teams make up a squad, which can have up to 10 soldiers including vehicle operators. In certain types of units, a squad may be called a section. A platoon combines three or four squads and up to 40 soldiers led by a lieutenant and platoon sergeant. A company contains three to five platoons and up to 200 soldiers led by a captain. Artillery battalions call company-sized units batteries, while armour and cavalry units call them troops. Battalions, the basic combat formation of the BCT, have four to six companies and up to 1,000 soldiers commanded by a lieutenant colonel. The armour and cavalry branches use the term squadron.

The US Army has a regimental system and tradition, but the frequent reorganisations of the late 20th and early 21st centuries have diminished tradition's importance somewhat. For example, an infantry regiment normally has three battalions, but these battalions are spread across different BCTs, usually within the same division. Soldiers might spend the bulk of a career in the same division, particularly within the airborne and air assault formations, but rarely will that career take place in the same BCT. This diminishes the tradition of regimental cohesiveness, a victim of modern military exigency.

However, each battalion retains its regimental traditions, including its colours, crest, and history. Soldiers typically take great pride in this affiliation, as it provides a sense of continuity to the past. Each battalion's soldiers will wear the regimental crest on their dress uniform, reinforcing their affiliation. Most battalions have mottos taught to every newly arrived recruit. And a few National Guard units can trace their origins to militia organisations which predate the creation of the United States.

For most soldiers, their real home is their squad and platoon. These are the soldiers they will live, train, and fight beside. The expanded parts of their units, the companies, battalions and larger, are important but more abstract. It is a truth of military service that in combat soldiers fight not for concepts such as patriotism or medals, but for each other. This makes the cohesion of small units vital, something the army strives constantly to build and maintain.

RIGHT: An infantry fire team moves through smoke to assault an objective during training at Fort Benning, Georgia. This team includes a light machine gunner, grenadier and rifleman also carrying an AT4 anti-tank weapon on his back. (US ARMY)

36 US ARMY YEARBOOK 2023

US ARMY YEARBOOK 2023

Training

Citizen to Soldier

LEFT: Drill sergeants wear distinctive campaign hats, also called 'covers', to identify them to recruits. They train soldiers in the basic skills needed to proceed to advanced training and then an active unit.
(US ARMY)

The United States Army never stops training its soldiers, from the day they enter the army until they reach the end of their term of service or, for a dedicated few, retire after a full career of 20 years or more. The desired result is a combat-ready force able to deploy anywhere in the world on short notice.

For enlisted soldiers it all begins with Basic Combat Training (BCT), conducted at one of four bases. Each base specialises in training soldiers for particular Military Occupational Specialities (MOS). For example, infantry and armour branch soldiers go to Fort Benning Georgia, while artillery recruits go to Fort Sill, Oklahoma. A soldier's MOS is decided based on available vacancies and the recruit's choice. At BCT soldiers learn to march, use military courtesies, fire and maintain basic small arms, and work as a team. After BCT, the new soldier moves on to Advanced Individual Training (AIT) where they take special training for their branch of service. A few specialities combine BCT and AIT into a single longer, more demanding course. The result is a soldier with the basic skills to join a unit.

Officers come to the army from a variety of sources, including the Military Academy at West Point, New York, various Reserve Officer's Training Corps (ROTC) units located at universities around the country, and the Officer Candidate School (OCS) at Fort Benning, Georgia. Most OCS attendees are serving enlisted soldiers who meet the educational requirements. A small number of officers come from private military academies. Officers attend branch specific schools soon after commissioning. For officers and NCOs to be promoted throughout their careers, they must attend various courses designed to educate and professionalise them as they mature. To attain ranks of lieutenant colonel and above, various advanced courses are required.

Units train together at their garrison bases, which are generally large enough for live fire ranges and limited field exercises. There is also a network of large training bases which allow brigades to manoeuvre under simulated combat conditions. These include the National Training Centre at Fort Irwin, California and the Joint Readiness Training Centre at Fort Polk, Louisiana. US Army units also regularly train with other branches of the US military and at overseas locations such as Grafenwoehr in Germany and Australia's Shoalwater Bay Military Training Area.

ABOVE: Ranger School is one of the toughest courses for an infantry soldier. Graduation confers status among their peers and the right to wear the Ranger tab on their uniform.
(US ARMY)

STRUCTURE

Brigade Combat Teams

Combined Arms Firepower

The Brigade Combat Team (BCT) is the basic fighting unit of the US Army. It is a balanced, combined arms force mixing battalions from different branches into a self-contained force capable of engaging in combat and sustaining itself during extended field operations. A brigade is generally the smallest unit which will be deployed on its own for major tasks and employs 4-5,000 soldiers.

There are five basic types of BCTs. The Armored BCT combines tank and mechanised infantry into combined arms battalions; the infantry are equipped with Bradley Fighting Vehicles for additional punch. Stryker Brigades are infantry formations using Stryker wheeled armoured vehicles, which are lighter and more mobile than the Bradley. Infantry brigades come in three forms: light infantry, airborne, and air assault. Airborne units employ paratroopers while air assault brigades utilise helicopters to move their troops around the battlefield. There are also two cavalry regiments which are functionally equivalent to Stryker BCTs but retain their traditional regimental designations.

Each BCT contains three infantry battalions, except for the armoured formations which have the mixed tank/infantry battalions. Each brigade also fields an artillery battalion, a cavalry squadron for reconnaissance, an engineer battalion and a brigade support battalion consisting of medical, maintenance and logistics companies. Many BCTs stationed outside the Continental United States (CONUS) are short one infantry battalion.

BCT commanders generally organise their battalions into task forces centred around a single infantry or armoured battalion, with attachments such as an artillery battery, medical platoon, engineer platoon and forward support company. In armoured BCTs, task forces will have a mix of tank and mechanised infantry for mutual support; this is reflected in the makeup of the combined arms battalions in each Armored BCT.

RIGHT: Brigades often conduct map exercises prior to an operation. This brings all the unit's officers together to ensure their understanding and improve coordination.
(US ARMY)

ABOVE: Troops of 2nd Brigade, 1st Cavalry Division set up a hasty command post during a training rotation at the National Training Center, California, where large units can manoeuvre.
(US ARMY)

US ARMY YEARBOOK 2023

Divisions, Corps and Armies

Ready for Action

Above brigades, the army organises into divisions, corps, and armies, often referred to as field armies to differentiate them from the US Army as a whole, nicknamed 'big army'. The regular army has 12 divisions, with eight more in the National Guard. These divisions are assigned to corps and field armies as needed. This structure is designed to be flexible, with headquarters at each level normally able to control from two to four subordinate units, though these numbers can vary.

The division oversees from two to four BCTs, plus aviation, field artillery, engineer, and logistics brigades. Divisions average about 16,000 soldiers and are commanded by a major general. While able to deploy and operate on its own, divisions usually operate under a higher-level headquarters, particularly since the US Army has regional headquarters, called commands, which cover the globe.

The corps as a tactical formation oversees from one to three divisions, and the term should not be confused with its more archaic use to describe large, formal organisations (i.e., the Corps of Engineers). Commanded by a lieutenant general, corps also have extra battalions and brigades in various specialties to add to its capabilities. This can include extra field artillery, signals, transportation, aviation, and logistics units, which can be used by the corps headquarters or attached as needed to its subordinate divisions to add to their combat power. A corps can have anywhere from 40,000 to 100,000 troops. Corps are traditionally numbered using Roman numerals. The current Corps are I, III, V and XVIII Airborne Corps.

The field armies would oversee two or more corps during active operations and would also have extra battalions and brigades under its control, similar to corps. If the army goes to war in any part of the world, the field army would assume command of the deployed forces. The numbered armies are generally assigned to regional army commands which are themselves subordinate to the joint commands controlled by the Department of Defence. For example, 7th Army is subordinate to US Army Europe and Africa, which falls under US European Command (EUCOM). An exception is First Army, based in the United States, which oversees mobilisation, training, and readiness.

LEFT: Officers of allied nations are often given command positions in American higher-echelon headquarters to improve understanding and interoperability. British Maj Gen Michael Keating served as the deputy commander of support for US III Corps at Fort Hood Texas, seen here in 2022 (US ARMY)

BELOW: Division and Corps headquarters are literal 'tent cities'. Any soldier who has served in one is familiar with the ritual of setting up and taking down these massive fabric structures. (US ARMY)

STRUCTURE

Order of Battle
Organised for War

ABOVE: M1A2 Tanks of the 1st ABCT, 1st Infantry Division, line up for an exercise at Bucierz Range, Poland. This brigade is part of the recently activated V Corps, the US Army's forward-deployed corps in Europe. (US ARMY)

BELOW: A 105mm cannon crew from the 319th Airborne Field Artillery Battalion during a fire support coordination exercise with Moroccan troops, designed to strengthen interoperability between the two nations. (US ARMY)

US Army Active-Duty Divisions and Brigade Combat Teams	
1st Armored Division (Fort Bliss Texas)	**1st Cavalry Division (Fort Hood, Texas)**
1st Armored Brigade Combat Team	1st Armored Brigade Combat Team
2nd Armored Brigade Combat Team	2nd Armored Brigade Combat Team
3rd Armored Brigade Combat Team	3rd Armored Brigade Combat Team
1st Infantry Division (Fort Riley, Kansas)	**2nd Infantry Division (Camp Humphreys, South Korea)**
1st Armored Brigade Combat Team	1 rotating Brigade Combat Team
2nd Armored Brigade Combat Team	
3rd Infantry Division (Fort Stewart, Georgia)	**4th Infantry Division (Fort Carson, Colorado)**
1st Armored Brigade Combat Team	1st Stryker Brigade Combat Team
2nd Armored Brigade Combat Team	2nd Stryker Brigade Combat Team
81st Stryker Brigade Combat Team**	3rd Armored Brigade Combat Team
7th Infantry Division (Joint Base Lewis-McChord, Washington) (Headquarters Only)	**10th Mountain Division (Fort Drum, New York)**
1st Stryker Brigade Combat Team	1st Infantry Brigade Combat Team
2nd Stryker Brigade Combat Team	2nd Stryker Brigade Combat Team
81st Stryker Brigade Combat Team**	86th Infantry Brigade Combat Team***
	3rd Infantry Brigade Combat Team****
11th Airborne Division (Joint base Elmendorf-Richardson, Alaska)	**25th Infantry Division (Schofield Barracks, Hawaii)**
1st Infantry Brigade Combat Team	2nd Infantry Brigade Combat Team
2nd Infantry Brigade Combat Team (Airborne)	3rd Infantry Brigade Combat Team
82nd Airborne Division (Fort Bragg, North Carolina)	**101st Airborne Division (Fort Campbell, Kentucky)**
1st Infantry Brigade Combat Team (Airborne)	1st Infantry Brigade Combat Team (Air Assault)
2nd Infantry Brigade Combat Team (Airborne)	2nd Infantry Brigade Combat Team (Air Assault)
3rd Infantry Brigade Combat Team (Airborne)	3rd Infantry Brigade Combat Team (Air Assault)
Separate Brigade Combat Teams:	
2nd Cavalry Regiment (Stryker) (Vilseck, Germany)	
3rd Cavalry Regiment (Stryker) (Fort Hood, Texas)	
173rd Airborne Brigade Combat Team (Vicenza, Italy)	
Additional supporting brigades not part of the above divisions include:	
2 Combat Aviation Brigades	3 Military Intelligence Brigades
5 Field Artillery Brigades	6 Air Defence Artillery Brigades
4 Engineer Brigades	2 Sustainment Brigades
5 Military Police Brigades	1 Transportation Brigade
5 Medical Brigades	9 Signal Brigades
1 Chemical Brigade	5 Security Force Assistance Brigades
Notes:	
- Each division also contains a headquarters element, divisional artillery, an engineer brigade, a combat aviation brigade and a sustainment brigade.	
* Attached from Georgia Army National Guard	
** Attached from Washington Army National Guard	
*** Attached from Vermont Army National Guard	
**** Stationed at Fort Polk, Louisiana	

US ARMY YEARBOOK 2023

The 915th Cyber Battalion

A new organisation for a new form of conflict

The information realm holds both threat and opportunity for the US Army. There remain many undefined rules around cyber activities. For example, there is still no consensus about how damaging a cyber-attack must be to constitute an act of war. Until an agreed-upon set of rules is instituted, military organisations must prepare for a broad range of threats, from small hacking attempts to attacks on national infrastructure.

The army seeks to achieve true multidomain capability, including the cyber realm. Toward this end, in 2019 it activated the 915th Cyber Battalion. While the stereotypical view of cyber operators puts them in a darkened room, staring into a computer screen amid empty energy drink cans, the 915th belies this misconception. The battalion trains and prepares for deployments alongside other army forces.

The 915th controls a growing (and unspecified) number of Expeditionary Cyber and electromagnetic activities Teams (ECTs). These teams provide a mix of cyber, electronic warfare and information operations capabilities to deployed units which require them. When an army force is sent overseas, it can request an ECT from the 915th. A ready team will be sent to that force and will train, deploy, and operate within their headquarters.

This allows forces in the field to have their own dedicated and local cyber capability, rather than having to call for assistance from an unconnected group which may be thousands of miles away. ECTs will normally align with a theatre-level headquarters.

A difficulty of cyber warfare is its ever-evolving nature. This requires ECTs to train constantly and stay abreast of new developments. This also means they are given latitude to experiment and develop new techniques. According to battalion Sergeant Major Marlene Harshman: "From the strategic operations to the tactical level, the requirements and the threats… constantly make it evolve. Doctrine, if you will, is, 'this is how you can do it.' Well, but what happens if this is how you can do it today but not how you do it tomorrow?"

LEFT: Cyber warfare requires connectivity to networks; antennas are becoming as common in the field as machine guns. (US ARMY)

ABOVE: Cyber warfare soldiers require specialised equipment to fulfil their role in the field. These NCOs are working in a modified Stryker armoured vehicle. (US ARMY)

www.keymilitary.com 41

A GLOBAL FORCE

The US Army Around the World

Worldwide presence, worldwide reach

RIGHT: US paratroopers fire a Stinger anti-aircraft missile during an air defence exercise in Croatia. The Stinger is an effective weapon against helicopters and low-flying aircraft.
(US ARMY)

BELOW: Engineers clear a path for a tank platoon. Kuwait has hosted US Army units for three decades, providing a base for operations throughout the Middle East.
(US ARMY)

The US Army's global responsibilities require it maintain an extensive network of bases, training areas, and support facilities. Due to security concerns and the rapid pace of operations, it is difficult to obtain a truly accurate count of exactly how many bases the army has overseas. Even many of its facilities within the United States are now termed 'joint bases', where personnel from all branches of the US military work and train together.

The US has sufficient military facilities within its borders to carry out most training requirements, even for entire brigades. These bases also contain a variety of terrain types including, desert, woodland, mountain, arctic and jungle. While it has its own training areas in Germany, most of the Army's overseas training sites are shared with host nations, such as South Korea, Bulgaria, and Kuwait. These bases allow US units to train with their allies on the same terrain they would experience in a real conflict. Allied nations frequently train at bases in the US as well.

Army units usually fulfil several roles when deployed outside the US. They provide forces in being, ready for immediate response to a crisis in their assigned region. They serve to deter potential adversaries from actions which would bring a full response from the US military. In places like Iraq and Syria, American troops are actively engaged in operations. While the stated mission there is to assist local governments in maintaining security until they can do so independently, US soldiers will occasionally need to defend themselves or act against regional adversaries such as so-called Islamic State (IS) splinter groups.

A clear example of a force in being is the Eighth Army, stationed in South Korea. Its primary purpose is to dissuade North Korea from invading South Korea. Eighth Army is the ground component of US Forces Korea (USFK). It is also a 'tripwire force', not large or well-equipped enough to ensure a defeat of North Korea, but sufficient to ensure attacking it will draw the United States into the conflict.

Another role is that of training. The US almost always operates as part of a coalition. When the Army must fight alongside allied forces, it wants those forces to be well-trained and professional. This gives American commanders an idea of what allied formations will be capable of in the event they must fight together. Training allied armies provides understanding and commonality among partners. When the ally is a nation with a capable and advanced army, such as the UK or Australia, the US Army still wants to train with them for better understanding. In these cases, US soldiers often state how much they learn during such exercises.

In Japan, the US Army presence is limited compared to the other service branches, but soldiers there operate the AN/TPY-2 radar, designed to detect ballistic missile launches and provide fire control support for missile defence systems in the Western Pacific. Various logistics, communication and headquarters units make up the rest of US Army, Japan (USARJ), able to support the arrival of forces from the United States in the event of renewed hostilities in Korea or elsewhere in the region.

By far the largest number of Army troops outside the Continental United States (CONUS) are present in Europe, mainly in Germany and Italy. This is a holdover from the Cold War; during that period US forces were assigned to southern Germany. This is still apparent when looking at a map of US facilities in Germany, as they are all still in the south. Gradually, more US troops are moving eastward into Poland, Romania and elsewhere to deter Russia from threatening NATO nations.

Finally, small numbers of US soldiers, usually no more than a few hundred and often many less, are posted throughout Africa and South America. Most of them provide training and liaison support to their host nations. Often these troops will be Special Forces contingents, as one of their main missions is to train and support allied militaries.

ABOVE: Paratroopers of the 173rd Airborne Brigade land on an Italian drop zone. Airborne units are lightly equipped but able to deploy rapidly. (US ARMY)

ABOVE: Global responsibilities mean strategic mobility. The US Army is well-practiced at moving its heavy units to critical points, like this M1 tank unloading from a ship at Gdynia, Poland in December 2022. (US ARMY)

BELOW: Europe continues to be a major focus for heavy units of the US Army. Here, a Bradly IFV of the 1st Cavalry Division fires a TOW missile at a range in Poland. (US ARMY)

ALLIED STRENGTH

US Army Partnerships

Allies around the globe

RIGHT: Kuwaiti and French forces take part in a joint military exercise in December 2022. Artillery, attack helicopters and fighter jets supported armoured forces on the ground. (US ARMY)

It is highly unlikely the US Army will enter a major conflict alone, nor does it want to. Allies are key to Army operations worldwide, even in peacetime. Where possible, the United States attempts to align its interests with those of other nations, prompting cooperation. For the US, the reason is simple. The United States is currently the dominant global power; one of its primary interests is ensuring no viable challengers arise and the only place that can feasibly happen is on the Eurasian landmass.

While the US can claim global dominance, its power, whether economic, political or military, is not supreme. To attain its goals, it must have allies within the regions where conflict is likely to occur. It also desires allies who are similarly interested in preventing the rise of powerful adversaries who could conquer or dominate them.

BELOW: American and Canadian paratroopers drop onto an Alaskan training area, before moving against an opposing force from the US 25th Infantry Division. (US ARMY)

Many of America's alliances stem from the global realities of the 20th century. The US entered World War Two to prevent Nazi Germany from becoming a global superpower which could rival it. Next, America struggled to stem the expansion and success of the Soviet Union during the Cold War. However, it carefully avoided direct conflict with the nuclear-armed Soviets while engaging in proxy wars when it felt obliged to do so.

In the 21st century, America is concerned with growing Chinese power and the fear of eventual aggression if China decides to use its new strength. A hostile Russia, while much weaker than the Soviet Union, still possesses thousands of nuclear weapons and despite mediocre performance in Ukraine, is far from helpless. Iran presents threats to the flow of oil from the Middle East, a major factor in the global economy. Finally, North Korea's military is obsolescent, but its small nuclear arsenal and unpredictable behaviour draw attention, which is likely the goal.

To frustrate the chance for conflict with any of these potential opponents, the US takes part in a system of alliances in which the US Army plays a major part. These alliances are only truly successful if they prevent war; warfare is unpredictable in its outcome and even a war which ends in victory is wasteful in terms of human life, money and expended power. If war comes, however, it is vital to achieve victory.

The US has, in effect, a worldwide alliance with the United Kingdom, Canada, Australia and New Zealand. The armies of these five nations are peers in terms of professionalism, overall quality, training and when working together, global reach. The national goals of each differ at times, but there is truth in the statement that if you go to war with one of these countries, you will eventually be at war with all of them.

The largest contingent of US Army troops is currently committed to NATO and the defence of Europe. This makes sense as any fighting between NATO and Russia would be a ground war where the Army already has a strong presence and extensive basing and infrastructure. There is unlikely to be a major reduction in US Army units in Europe while the Ukraine War continues.

In the Indo-Pacific, the US is expanding an already broad network of alliances to contain Chinese expansion, much in the way America 'surrounded' the Soviet Union to the east, west and south during the Cold War. To China's east, the US Army fosters partnerships with Japan and South Korea, which are equally effective against North Korea. To the southeast, the US Army is active in training with the Philippines, Thailand, Singapore and is improving relations with its Cold War enemy, Vietnam. On China's southern flank, India, while generally walking a path of non-alignment, does train with the US Army, recognising that in the event of war with China, America is a potential ally.

In the Middle East, the US Army has a much-reduced troop presence than during the wars in Iraq and Afghanistan but keeps contingents of soldiers carrying out training and coordination tasks in various countries including Kuwait, Bahrain, the United Arab Emirates, Jordan and Qatar. Much of the region is within range of Iranian missiles and UAVs, making air defence exercises common along with long range artillery drills. Jordan and Bahrain both operate the M142 HIMARS system; joint exercises with American HIMARS-equipped artillery units are frequent.

LEFT: Colombian commandos meet with US Gen Laura Richardson, commander of US Southern Command. (US ARMY)

BELOW: An American paratrooper rappels from a Ukrainian helicopter during a 2021 exercise. Prior to the Russian invasion, US and NATO troops regularly trained there. (US ARMY)

ABOVE: US and Australian troops train together in Indonesia during a 14-nation field exercise, Operation Pathways. (US ARMY)

BRANCHES

The Queen of Battle, follow me!

At the Heart of the Army

RIGHT: Infantrymen in Syria patrol near an oil refinery in 2020. These soldiers are part of a joint task force dedicated to keeping the so-called Islamic State (IS) from regaining power in the country. The M2 Bradley in the background prominently displays an American flag to identify the force and prevent inadvertent combat with Russian troops also operating in Syria.
(US ARMY)

The infantry branch fulfils the basic purpose of the army, providing soldiers able to take and hold ground and defeat opponents in close combat. The infantry is known as the 'Queen of Battle'; the most popular theory on the origin of this name relates to the queen on a chessboard, who enjoys far more mobility than other pieces. The infantry's motto is 'Follow Me', as they lead the way in battle. Their symbol is a pair of crossed muskets.

Infantry Brigade Combat Teams (IBCTs) are the backbone of the army's combat force. Each BCT has three battalions of infantry with attached artillery and support units as needed. The exception are the infantry units in armoured brigades, where tank and mechanised infantry companies are mixed into combined arms battalions. These infantry soldiers use the heavy Bradley Fighting Vehicle to carry them to the battlefield and provide firepower support with its cannon, antitank missiles, and machine gun.

Stryker brigades are also mechanised infantry but use the eight-wheeled Stryker combat vehicle as transport. The Stryker is not as well protected as the heavier Bradley but is faster and more easily transported to a conflict area. Stryker brigades were active in Iraq and Afghanistan where they adapted well to the relatively poor infrastructure. They are a little larger than armoured brigades and cost about the same to maintain, about $3 billion per year.

Regular infantry brigades are often called 'light' IBCTs and come in several forms. Standard IBCTs employ infantry in their traditional role as footsoldiers. Sometimes they will have focused training for particular environments, such as the 10th Mountain Division's IBCTs. Jungle warfare is an area of expertise for the 25th Infantry Division, which is the army's major combat unit in the Pacific Command (PACOM), although the Asia-Pacific region's vast size could see soldiers fighting anywhere from jungle-covered islands to the frozen mountains of the Korean peninsula.

Airborne brigades are just that; they use paratroopers capable of making parachute drops into combat zones on short notice and with little support. They are ideal for short, sharp attacks behind enemy lines but lack the endurance or heavy firepower for extended fighting. They must be quickly relieved by heavier ground forces and may need resupply by air if that relief is delayed. Despite this drawback, airborne units tend to draw aggressive recruits and are known for their offensive spirit. There are currently five airborne brigades, three under the 82nd Airborne Division, one stationed in Italy, and another in Alaska. Prospective paratroopers must pass a three-week airborne school at Fort Benning, Georgia; success confers the right to wear an airborne badge on their uniform.

The Immediate Response Force (IRF) is tasked to be able to deploy anywhere in the world within 18 hours of receiving orders to move. One brigade of the 82nd Airborne is rotated through this position every six months. Since being created in 2018, the IRF has been deployed three times, once each to Iraq and Afghanistan, and once to Washington DC during a civil disturbance.

The three Air Assault IBCTs of the 101st Airborne Division (Air Assault) specialise in the use of helicopters for battlefield mobility. The division has extra aviation assets under its control to facilitate this capability. The unit operates a school to teach its troops the essentials of heliborne operations, such as rappelling, sling-loading equipment beneath heavy lift helicopters such as the CH47 Chinook and how to make fast attacks and battlefield movements using their helicopters. Qualified air assault soldiers wear an air assault badge on their uniform, a pair of wings with a helicopter between them. Air »

ABOVE: This paratrooper has just landed on a drop zone near Fort Greely, Alaska and is uncasing his M240 machine gun. He is taking part in a Joint Forcible Entry Operation which will end with a live fire exercise. (US ARMY)

LEFT: Infantrymen disembark from UH60 Blackhawk helicopters during an air assault exercise in Kuwait. Air assault brigades combine infantry firepower with mobility and enable rapid movement around the battlefield. (NEEDS CREDIT)

BRANCHES

RIGHT: Two lieutenants hold their rifles overhead as they enter a water pit. They are preparing to attend Ranger School, one of the Army's toughest infantry courses, with a failure rate as high as 75%. (PENNSYLVANIA NG)

ABOVE: Infantry soldiers train in a wide variety of climates to instil physical and mental toughness. Soldiers could be deployed on short notice anywhere from Middle Eastern deserts to arctic tundra. (US ARMY)

soldiers wear an air assault badge on their uniform, a pair of wings with a helicopter between them. Air assault schools are periodically put on by other units, to increase soldier skills and provide cadres of troops skilled in helicopter operations. Any infantry unit could in theory operate via helicopters, making this a sensible practice.

All infantry units are assigned trucks and other wheeled vehicles for basic transport and logistical support. Depending on the situation, IBCTs can have additional vehicles assigned to them to increase their mobility, protection, and effectiveness. This often includes Mine Resistant, Ambush Protected vehicles (MRAPs), thousands of which were acquired by the army during the wars in Iraq and Afghanistan.

The Army's most elite infantry force is the 75th Ranger Regiment, a light infantry unit composed of three battalions with support troops. The regiment currently serves in the US military's Special Operation Command (SOCOM) where it supports 'high-tier' Special Forces units or conducts independent assignments as needed.

Infantry basic training is conducted at Fort Benning, Georgia. Courses for infantry officers are also taught here. The Ranger School is headquartered at Fort Benning, though training is carried out at several posts around the country. Graduates of Ranger School wear a tab with the word 'Ranger' on their sleeve above their unit patch. The school is arduous, and graduates gain a measure of respect for completing it. It is expected a career infantry officer will graduate Ranger School early in their service.

The Army's ceremonial unit is the 3rd Infantry Regiment, based at Fort Myer, Virginia, near Washington DC. Its duties include guarding the Tomb of the Unknown Soldier at Arlington National Cemetery, funeral escort, and escorting the president during ceremonies around the nation's capital. The unit also conducts normal infantry training, as it is assigned to defend the city during emergencies or civil disturbances.

Armour

The combat arm of decision

After acquiring small numbers of British and French tanks during World War One, the US Army's tank force atrophied after the war ended. This continued until the late 1930s, when the looming second global conflict forced the army's leadership to modernise. The tank has figured prominently in the American military ever since. American tanks during 1939-45 were known for being reliable and sturdy but lacked the firepower and armour protection of the opposing German panzers. Post-war, the army strived to ensure its tanks never again lacked the ability to face enemy tanks on at least even terms.

The M-1 Abrams is the culmination of that effort. It is at least as good as any tank it is likely to face in battle and superior to almost all of them. It compares very favourably with the most advanced tanks of allied powers, such as the excellent British Challenger, German Leopard II and French LeClerc. These tanks are so close in their capabilities that which is best is a source of conjecture best discussed over an evening pint in a warm pub!

Armed with the M-1 Abrams, the M2 Bradley Infantry Fighting Vehicle (IFV), the M3 Cavalry Fighting Vehicle (CFV) and M1126 Stryker, the US Army's armour branch proclaims itself as the 'Combat Arm of Decision'. Armour provides the heavy punch needed to smash through enemy lines, quickly drive into their rear areas and cause havoc. The concentrated firepower of an armoured unit, combined with its mobility and heavy protection make it a fearsome tool for heavy combat.

This awesome ability was best shown in the 1991 Gulf War and the initial invasion of Iraq in 2003. During the Gulf War over 1,800 Abrams tanks ranged across the desert taking a heavy toll of Iraqi armoured vehicles. None were destroyed by enemy fire, though a handful were lost to friendly fire incidents. In 2003 the Abrams faced fewer Iraqi tanks but still proved far superior to their opponents. Some were knocked out during close fighting with enemy infantry and insurgents, though most were

BELOW: The muzzle flash of the 120mm cannon is considerable; in combat tanks generally move to alternate positions immediately after shooting to avoid return fire. (US ARMY)

BRANCHES

ABOVE: The Bradley has been the US Army's primary IFV for four decades. These vehicles are involved in a training exercise in Latvia during Operation Atlantic Resolve. (US ARMY)

RIGHT: Each day a tank crew must refresh their camouflage with local flora, mixed with netting and the always present dust thrown up by the tracks. (US ARMY)

RIGHT: Restocking with ammunition is a frequent part of a tank crew's life in the field. The ammunition is stored in special compartments with blast panels to reduce the chance of a catastrophic explosion if the tank is hit. (US ARMY)

repaired and put back into service. Improvised Explosive Devices proved a more serious threat, which were countered with upgrades to the tank's armour protection.

As time went by in Iraq, tanks saw less use as the war slowly ended. The US Army did not deploy tanks to Afghanistan. Additionally, new anti-tank weapons have entered service in the 21st century which make the tank more vulnerable. This led pundits to proclaim the era of the tank was over, with the heavy vehicles simply too big a target to survive on modern battlefields.

This claim had been made before, but with the Ukraine war and new security threats in Europe the armour branch is experiencing a renaissance. Tanks are playing a major role in that conflict, despite the Russians taking heavy losses due to poor tactics and training. Properly utilised and maintained, armour is still a war-winning weapon. US armour is present in NATO battlegroups currently forward deployed in Eastern Europe.

The primary unit of the armour branch is the Armored Brigade Combat Team (ABCT). It contains three Combined Arms Battalions, each with three companies of either tanks or mechanised infantry. Each battalion will have either two tank companies and one mechanised infantry company, or one of tanks and two of infantry. Each company will have either 14 tanks or IFVs, as appropriate. This organisation resembles the mutually supporting tank-infantry task forces US armoured units used in World War Two. The brigade also has artillery, support and engineer battalions, and a cavalry squadron for reconnaissance.

The cavalry is part of the armour branch, and it should be noted that in American units, a troop is a company-sized element equivalent to a British squadron, while the American squadron is akin to a UK regiment. A US Cavalry squadron contains three reconnaissance troops equipped with the M3 CFV, a modified Bradley IFV. It also has a tank company and a headquarters element. Cavalry squadrons contain fewer personnel than an infantry battalion but have significant firepower due to their various armoured vehicles. US doctrine assumes the cavalry may have to fight to obtain needed information.

The armour branch is based at Fort Benning, Georgia, where both armour and infantry soldiers are trained. Its symbol is the outline of a Cold War-era M26 Pershing tank in front of two crossed sabres. Many armour and cavalry soldiers wear dark blue 19th-century cavalry hats, similar to a cowboy hat, for ceremonies and special events.

LEFT: In the field IFVs are soon covered with various bits of kit, ammunition, tools, and soldier's personal items. (US ARMY)

BELOW: This tank unit of the Montana National Guard is about to conduct a live fire exercise during training in Jordan in September 2022. Note the recovery vehicle and medical carrier standing by in case of accident or breakdown. (US ARMY)

BRANCHES

Field Artillery

King of Battle

RIGHT: The AN/TPQ-53 radar detects and classifies incoming mortar, cannon and rocket fire and reports both launch and impact locations. It can be operated remotely via cable from up to a kilometre away. (US ARMY)

BELOW: The M777 is the army's heavy towed gun. These artillerymen of the 3rd Cavalry Regiment fire on so-called Islamic State (IS) fighters in support of Iraqi and Coalition troops in 2018. (US ARMY)

While the infantry branch of the army is known as the Queen of Battle, the artillery is the undisputed king, a nod to its supreme ability to cause casualties on the battlefield. It is also the army's oldest branch, as its oldest unit is the Ancient and Honorable Artillery Company of Massachusetts, which still performs honorary duties. Artillery soldiers are known as 'Redlegs,' in reference to the red stripes on the 19th century artillerymen's uniform trousers. The current badge of the branch is a pair of crossed cannons.

Modern field artillery uses a wide variety of weapons and equipment: cannon, rockets, missiles, target acquisition radars, and drones are all part of artillery inventory. Most units are organised into battalions which function as direct support to the infantry and armour in Brigade Combat Teams. The artillery battalions in light infantry, airborne and air assault brigades use the M119 105mm and M777 155mm towed guns. Stryker Brigades use the M777, while armoured brigades are issued with the M109A6 or A7 Paladin 155mm self-propelled howitzer. Direct support battalions also use forward observers to locate targets.

The remaining artillery battalions, equipped variously with cannon or rocket/missile launchers are organised into Field Artillery Brigades (FABs) assigned at the corps or army level, providing general and reinforcing support to combat units. FAB headquarters elements are further able to coordinate the activities of multiple battalions in concert with close air support, attack helicopters, electronic warfare assets and other capabilities to create synergistic effects on the battlefield.

The FAB also contains a target acquisition battery using radar systems able to detect enemy projectiles in flight and calculate their firing points of origin so counterbattery fire can be directed at it. A UAV battery uses drones to locate targets as well. A signal company and support battalion perform communications and logistics duties for the FAB. Most of the army's FABs are in the National Guard, as study has determined reserve component soldiers can effectively perform these duties even with the reduced training time available to them.

Fort Sill, Oklahoma is the home of the field artillery branch. New artillery soldiers attend initial training and the advanced artillery schools are located there. The schools here also train members of the Marine Corps and students from allied militaries across the globe.

BELOW: Forward observers locate targets and direct artillery fire onto them from the front lines. This paratrooper directs fire using a lightweight laser designator/rangefinder during a **NATO** exercise in Poland. (US ARMY)

The M109A7 is the Army's newest self propelled howitzer. Here, members of the North Carolina National Guard test fire their newly issued weapons in 2021. (US ARMY)

BRANCHES

Aviation

Helicopters for transport, cargo, scouting and attack

RIGHT: UAVs are a natural addition to aviation units. These technicians perform last minute checks on an RQ7 Shadow before flight. (US ARMY)

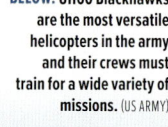

BELOW: UH60 Blackhawks are the most versatile helicopters in the army and their crews must train for a wide variety of missions. (US ARMY)

Aviation assumed a major role in the US Army during the Vietnam conflict, when helicopter designs became mature enough to perform effectively in multiple roles. Since then, the aviation branch's Combat Aviation Brigade (CAB) has become an indispensable part of the Army's structure. The Army's aircraft are almost entirely helicopters, or 'rotary wing' aircraft, as an agreement with the US Air Force reserves the use of regular, or 'fixed wing' aircraft to that service. The army operates only a few hundred fixed wing planes, mostly for specialised transport, such as moving general officers and important persons, and for special electronic surveillance and reconnaissance.

Most of the Army's helicopter models are legacy designs. The Apache and Blackhawk entered service in the early 1980s while the Chinook has been in army use since the 1960s. It is a testament to their design that all three have proven durable and able to be upgraded throughout decades of combat use.

The CAB is the basic aviation unit of the Army. Each contains four battalions (sometimes called squadrons) of aircraft. The two attack/reconnaissance battalions use 48 Apaches and a dozen Shadow drones. The Assault Battalion flies 30 Blackhawks for troop and cargo

LEFT: Combat Aviation Brigades fly an assortment of attack, cargo, and utility helicopters, all of which can be armed for offensive or defensive needs. In this image, Chinook, Blackhawk, and Apache helicopters fly in formation during aerial gunnery qualification at Grafenwöhr, Germany. (US ARMY)

transport. The General Support battalion uses 12 Chinooks and 20 Blackhawks for heavy lift, medical evacuation and command and control. An attached company uses 12 Gray Eagle drones, and a fifth battalion contains the brigade's logistics assets. Each division has a CAB to provide comprehensive aviation support. CABs in the National Guard also fly the UH72 Lakota utility helicopter.

One notable addition is the 160th Special Operations Aviation Regiment (SOAR), which provides helicopter support to Special Forces units throughout the US military. This unit flies modified Blackhawks and Chinooks along with MH/AH6 Little Birds, nicknamed the 'killer egg' due to its distinctive hull shape.

The home of Army aviation is Fort Rucker, Alabama. Here, commissioned and warrant officers learn to fly and to operate an aviation unit. The branch insignia is a propeller flanked by a pair of wings.

LEFT: Regular maintenance is vital for keeping aircraft flying. Crews train to perform maintenance tasks in field environments. (US ARMY)

LEFT: The AH64 Apache fills both the attack and reconnaissance roles within Combat Aviation Brigades. This Apache is about to simulate an attack while an older OH58 Kiowa Observer-Controller aircraft oversees the exercise. (US ARMY)

BRANCHES

Combat Engineers

Cutting edge of the Army's sword

RIGHT: The ground shakes as sappers blow a hole through concertina wire during a training exercise at Fort Campbell, Kentucky. Wire obstacles are usually destroyed using Bangalore torpedoes, a section of pipe containing explosives, in use since World War Two. (US ARMY)

RIGHT: Obstacle breaching includes gaining entry into defended buildings. This engineer uses a 12-gauge shotgun to destroy the hinges on a doorframe during training (INDIANA NG)

BELOW: Combat engineers clear a road using mine detectors during a NATO exercise in Poland, September 2022. After finding the mine they must then disable or destroy it. (US ARMY)

Combat engineers are a key part of the Army's combat forces. They clear obstacles, create field fortifications such as trenches or tank scrapes, clear minefields and build bridges. Every BCT in the army has an engineer company within its organisation. There are also independent engineer brigades which are attached to corps or field army-sized formations to provide extra capability when deployed.

In the US Army, engineer soldiers are generally referred to as Combat Engineers to denote their strictly military role. This is because the army contains another organisation, the US Army Corps of Engineers, which carries out civil engineering projects around the United States and occasionally overseas. While some members of the Corps of Engineers are uniformed military personnel, most of its workforce are civilians.

Combat engineer units within BCTs specialise in roles immediately useful on the battlefield. These include both emplacing and clearing mines using a variety of detection and demolition equipment. They create defensive positions for friendly troops and penetrate those used by the enemy, referred to as 'breaching'. These engineers also deploy bridges for smaller rivers. To this end they are issued specialised armoured vehicles such as the XM1150 Assault Breacher Vehicle and the M9 Armored Combat Earthmover (ACE), essentially an armoured bulldozer. They also use MRAPs equipped with engineer

equipment including robots for clearing mines and Improvised Explosive Device (IEDs). Combat engineers are trained to fight as infantry in emergencies.

For larger tasks, the independent engineer brigades enter the field. They can emplace bridges over larger rivers, install fuel pipelines, water purification sites, build roads or airfields, and other things vital to an army on campaign.

The term Sapper is often applied to engineer soldiers, but in the US army it is a title given only to engineers who have passed a special course and proved their skills in a wide variety of engineering tasks. These soldiers are entitled to wear a tab on their uniform sleeve inscribed with the word 'Sapper.'

Combat engineers are trained at Fort Leonard Wood, Missouri. Their insignia is a castle with three towers.

US ARMY YEARBOOK 2023

Signal Corps

Communications and networks

Success in modern warfare requires widely separated units, often of different types, to be able to plan, coordinate and execute military operations with precise timing and information sharing. The Signal Corps ensures that capability. Without effective command and control army forces quickly lose their effectiveness. With it, their capabilities combine to become more than the simple sum of their weapons and personnel.

The Signal Corps was established in 1860, on the eve of the American Civil War. In the beginning signal flags, torches and telegraphy were its primary tools; even hot air balloons saw service to increase visual range. As technology advanced, telephones and radios became the primary means of communication. The modern Signal Corps is also responsible for satellite communications (though not the satellites, which are controlled by the US Air Force), data networks, internet and intranet systems and microwave communications equipment use.

Currently, Signal Brigades are testing small drones to improve line of sight communications with Unmanned Aerial Vehicles. Balloons equipped with communications gear are also undergoing field testing to improve the ability of combat units to operate against peer adversaries who can effectively jam satellite signals.

When units are deployed, signals soldiers are among the busiest troops in any headquarters element. Each time the headquarters emplaces, these soldiers must set up numerous radios, antennas, satellite dishes, internet protocol telephones, and computer systems. When the unit moves, all this equipment must be disconnected, broken down and packed for transport. In between, they work long hours keeping all these items functioning; modern electronic equipment can be sensitive, and any loss of communications means delays, confusion and possibly danger for frontline soldiers.

LEFT: A group of satellite communication maintainer/operators set up a network dish antenna. Satellite dishes are now a ubiquitous feature of military units. (US ARMY RESERVE)

Every army headquarters element, battalion or larger, has a signals section to provide support to that unit. These are led by a qualified signals officer with support from NCOs, all trained to analyse communications problems and remedy them. Separate Signal Brigades also exist to provide added capacity to corps and army-sized elements. Signal soldiers and officers attend their advanced training at Fort Gordon, Georgia. The symbol of the Signal Corps is a torch flanked by two signal flags.

BELOW: Radios such as this backpack unit are still the primary means of communication for soldiers in the field. (US ARMY)

BRANCHES

Combat Support

Direct Assistance to the frontline troops

The Army's combat arms include the infantry, artillery, armour, engineer, and aviation branches. While they provide the raw fighting power, their abilities are enhanced by four other arms which provide close assistance, deploying alongside or close to the combat troops. These branches are known as Combat Support. They are generally not expected to take a leading role in frontline fighting, though their proximity to the enemy means they may have to join the action in emergencies.

The Military Police (MPs) have a law enforcement function to enforce military laws and orders and arrest violators. When not deployed these troops often provide such services to their garrisons. When deployed, they also collect and guard enemy prisoners of war, direct traffic along major military routes, escort convoys, and secure important sites and road routes. Military police also patrol rear areas and conduct search operations for insurgents and enemy stragglers. In the National Guard, MPs may aid civilian police during civil disturbances.

The Military Intelligence Corps collects, interprets, and disseminates information on the enemy. This enables staff sections in combat units to plan operations with the benefit of knowledge about the size, equipment, and probable plans of the opposing forces. This information can be collected through interrogation of captured enemy soldiers, interception of radio or digital communications or interviews with local civilians. They also gather information from various sensor systems such as camera feeds from drones, radar, and reconnaissance platforms. Analysts then interpret the raw data, draw conclusions, and create estimates of enemy forces and abilities. Soldiers generally refer to this branch by the initials 'MI.'

The Chemical Corps is responsible for defending army forces against Chemical, Biological, Radiological and Nuclear (CBRN) threats. Essentially, the Chemical Corps deals with weapons of mass destruction. They prepare defensive plans based on knowledge of enemy capabilities, employ specialised devices to detect CBRN threats and operate decontamination equipment. Soldiers in this branch also learn how to handle hazardous materials safely. This branch has a secondary mission to provide covering smoke to combat units. Their standard vehicle for this role is the M58 Wolf, a converted M113 personnel carrier fitted with a large smoke generator. The Army is currently testing a robotic version of this vehicle.

The fourth Combat Support branch is the Signal Corps, covered on page 57.

ABOVE: Soldiers from a military intelligence battalion attempt to intercept low level enemy voice transmissions during a training exercise. Gathering useful information about the enemy is the 'MI's' core role (WASHINGTON NG)

LEFT: The Chemical Corps defends against nuclear, biological, and chemical attacks. Here, American and Japanese soldiers decontaminate a vehicle during an exercise on Okinawa in May 2022. (US ARMY)

US ARMY YEARBOOK 2023

Few know it, but the US Army maintains a considerable fleet of transport vessels. Here, the Logistics Support Vessel *General Brehon B. Somervell* takes part in a training exercise at Darwin Australia. (US ARMY)

Sustainment

Keeping soldiers fed, paid and their equipment working

Their work isn't glamourous, it receives scant attention, but without the work of the sustainment echelon, the army grinds to a halt. These are the soldiers who work in the rear of the battle area and at bases, ensuring everything the combat forces need to be effective is cared for and available. Formerly known as Combat Service Support, the sustainment branches include:

The Quartermaster Corps, charged with handling the general supply needs of the army, including food, water, fuel, and distribution of required supplies to the field forces, with the exception of ammunition and medical supplies. This branch also oversees mortuary affairs.

The Ordnance Corps provides weapons and ammunition. They support the development, acquisition, and production of these items along with training soldiers to maintain them. This means every weapon system in military service has soldiers specially trained to keep it serviceable under use.

The Transportation Corps' motto is 'Nothing Happens Until Something Moves'. This branch is responsible for movement of army troops wherever they are deployed. Toward this end it operates a wide variety of trucks, boats and even ships, including large ocean-going transports capable of lifting armoured vehicles. It is a little-known fact that the US Army Transportation Corps possesses more boats and ships (approximately 500) than the navies of most nations.

The Army Medical Department trains and supplies the army with doctors, nurses, dentists, veterinarians, and medical administrative personnel. It provides for the healthcare of both the active and reserve components.

The Adjutant General's Corps is the administrative hub of the army. It provides human resources services, oversees recruitment and retention, organises replacement soldiers for those who become casualties, and manages postal and recreation facilities. The 'AG' also oversees the army's band.

The Finance Corps is responsible for payroll and financial oversight of funds to ensure they are being used appropriately. Rarely considered day to day, most soldiers only think of this branch when there is a problem, such as pay not arriving.

Despite their status as 'rear-echelon' troops, their day-to-day efforts allow the rest of the army to concentrate on its job to engage and defeat the nation's enemies. Without the sustainment forces, the average infantryman would be left hungry, unpaid, unarmed, sick and with only their feet to carry them forward.

LEFT: Fuel is the lifeblood of mechanised forces. This petroleum supply specialist is setting up a Forward Aerial Refuelling Point (FARP) for a helicopter unit at Fort Carson, Colorado. (US ARMY)

BRANCHES

Special Forces

Unconventional warfare and special operations

ABOVE: The 160th SOAR's helicopters are specifically fitted to support Special Forces missions. These Green Berets are boarding as MH-60 Blackhawk during training in Alaska. (US ARMY)

RIGHT: Special Forces selection is a gruelling series of tests designed to ensure only the best candidates earn the coveted green beret and proceed to an active unit. (US ARMY)

The US Army's Special Forces occupy an unusual position, as they are operationally under the control of Special Operations Command (SOCOM), a joint organisation overseeing elite units from across the US military, including the Navy's Sea-Air-Land (SEAL) teams, the Marine Corps' Raider Regiments and Air Force Special Operations. SOCOM's goal is to coordinate the activities of these disparate groups into well-executed operations in support of national goals. SOCOM arose after the failed rescue attempt of American hostages held in Iran in 1979-81, to avoid a repeat of such a disaster.

The 75th Ranger Regiment is the initial echelon of Army Special Operations personnel and for many, the pathway into Special Forces and other elite SOCOM tiers. The Rangers are elite light infantry, parachute-qualified, with expertise in classic light infantry functions such as reconnaissance and ambush. Each Ranger must be a graduate of the Ranger School, headquartered at Fort Benning, Georgia. This school has an average failure rate of 60%, meaning only the most dedicated and skilled win the right to wear the Ranger Tab on their sleeve and the tan beret which is their distinctive headgear.

Special Forces soldiers, known as the Green Berets due to the colour of their headgear, are the equivalent of the UK's Special Air Service (SAS). Like the SAS, they are experts at unconventional warfare. While fully able to carry out what are known as 'direct action' missions, much of »

LEFT: Cooperation with friendly and allied groups is a major part of Special Forces duties. Here, Green Berets from the Ohio National Guard throw smoke grenades during an exercise with the US State Department's Diplomatic Security Service. (US ARMY)

Special Forces helicopters are often painted a non-reflective black colour since they operate almost exclusively at night. (USAF)

BRANCHES

their time is spent training friendly nation's soldiers and insurgents fighting America's enemies. However, such work often brings them into contact with hostile forces. In January 2018, a Special Forces team working with Syrian anti-government forces fought off an attack by government forces led by Russian mercenaries from the Wagner Group, inflicting an estimated 40% casualties.

The path to donning the green beret begins at the John F. Kennedy Special Warfare Centre and School at Fort Bragg, North Carolina. Here, prospective recruits must pass the Special Forces Qualification Course, known as the 'Q Course'. This gruelling programme has a 75% failure rate. It includes training in foreign languages, planning, survival, escape and many other necessary skills. Depending on their speciality, the full period of training can take up to two years. If the candidate succeeds, they are assigned to a 12-man Operation Detachment A, also known as an A Team.

From there, training continues with various advanced courses including sniper and scuba training. Green Berets train constantly when not on operations. As hard as the training programme is, the real challenge lies in becoming a successful member of their respective unit. There are five Special Forces Groups in the regular army, each equivalent to a brigade of 3-4 battalions with support elements. The National Guard maintains two more Special Forces groups.

Each Special Forces group is assigned a geographic area in which it will primarily operate. Green Berets learn languages and cultures common to their group's region. Special Forces receives extensive discretion on choosing specific weapons, vehicles, and other equipment needed to accomplish its mission.

In accordance with their mission of working with allied nation's forces, these groups are supported by Psychological Operations and Civil Affairs troops. A major addition to Army Special Forces is the 160th Special Operations Aviation Regiment (SOAR). This unit, known as the 'Night Stalkers', provides specialised helicopter support. All members of the 160th are volunteers and undergo their own focused training before attaining full membership.

US Army Special Forces		
Group	Basing	Geographical Focus
1st Special Forces Group	Ft. Lewis, Washington and Okinawa, Japan	Pacific Region
3rd Special Forces Group	Fort Bragg, North Carolina	Sub-Saharan Africa
5th Special Forces Group	Fort Campbell, Kentucky	Middle East, Central Asia
7th Special Forces Group	Eglin Air Force Base, Florida	Latin America, Caribbean
10th Special Forces Group	Fort Carson, Colorado and Stuttgart, Germany	Europe, North Africa
19th Special Forces Group – National Guard	Utah, Colorado, West Virginia	Southeast Asia, Pacific
20th Special Forces Group – National Guard	Alabama, Mississippi, Florida	Latin America

ABOVE: A primary role for Special Forces is training soldiers from allied nations. This Green Beret is teaching pistol marksmanship to Botswanan Defence Force commandoes. (NORTH CAROLINA NG)

A trio of Rangers engage the enemy in Afghanistan. The Rangers form the basis of US Army special operations forces. (US ARMY)

US Army Reserve

Vital support in war and peace

RIGHT: Half the Army's medical units are in the reserve. These reservists are going through a simulated mass casualty exercise. (US ARMY RESERVE)

RIGHT: Civil affairs soldiers are trained to collaborate with civil authorities in nations hosting US forces. These soldiers are practicing refugee movement control with the German Red Cross. (US ARMY RESERVE)

The US Army cannot effectively operate without activating its reserve components. This was an intentional decision by army leaders in the aftermath of the Vietnam conflict. That conflict, fought almost entirely by regular army units using conscripts, proved deeply divisive to the nation. Afterward the service reorganised so that certain types of units existed primarily in the Reserve and National Guard (see next page). This meant the army could not effectively deploy for a major conflict without activating the reserves. Since such an activation seriously affects the nation's workforce, economy, and cultural life, it was hoped the army would then only go to war when a majority of the citizenry supported doing so.

As such, the Army Reserve contains nearly all the service's civil affairs and psychological operations units, fully half the medical units, and a quarter of its military police. The reserve also fields large numbers of quartermaster, transportation, engineer, and military intelligence units. An army at war cannot function without the sort of logistical and technical support that reserve units supply.

Notably, there is only one combat arms unit in the Army Reserve. This was another intentional choice; combat units such as infantry, armour and artillery are assigned to the Regular Army and National Guard. The only exception is the 100th Infantry Battalion, originally part of the 442nd Infantry Regiment. During World War Two this unit was made up of American soldiers of Japanese ancestry who volunteered despite the discrimination they faced. It developed a reputation for bravery and determination in the European theatre, so this battalion was retained for historical reasons. This battalion is currently assigned in the Pacific region and has soldiers from Hawaii, Guam, American Samoa, and the West Coast of the US mainland.

Besides support units, the Army Reserve hosts three training commands with ten training divisions between them. If the United States were to enter a major war requiring it to expand quickly, these training units would be activated to prepare the tens of thousands of new recruits and conscripts for service. They would also provide refresher training to members of the Individual Ready Reserve (IRR). These are soldiers who have left active duty but did not elect to serve in the Reserve or National Guard; they are liable for recall up to eight years after they initially joined the army.

BRANCHES

The National Guard

Citizen Soldiers

BELOW: This Kentucky National Guard soldier is being trained to deal with firebombs during civil disturbance training in 2022. Note the plastic riot shield and the older pattern uniform, likely worn to avoid ruining his current clothing issue.
(US ARMY)

The second part of the US Army's reserve components is the National Guard. While the Army Reserve is controlled and run by the federal government, the National Guard is run by the individual states. Each state controls its own National Guard force, named for that state. For example, the California Army National Guard. The word army is included in the name to differentiate it from the Air National Guard, which is a state-run reserve component of the US Air Force. This division of military resources between the federal and state governments is a peculiarity of the United States' history of using militia forces for the bulk of its army. Guard units are also present in US territories, such as Guam, Puerto Rico, and Samoa.

Each state's National Guard falls under the control of the state governor, an elected civilian position. In practice, military commanders are drawn from the ranks of each

RIGHT: A New Jersey National Guardsman adjusts the fuses on 105mm howitzer ammunition. Over half of the Army's artillery units are in the National Guard.
(NEW JERSEY NG)

state's serving officers. Both enlisted and commissioned personnel attend the same training schools as the regular army, returning home afterward to join their unit. Once in a unit, the standard term of service is one weekend a month and a two-week training period, usually in the summer months. It is common for National Guardsmen, particularly the officers and NCOs, to serve extra days beyond the minimum requirement.

Beyond regular military duties, National Guardsmen are also trained to respond to civil emergencies, such as riots and natural disasters. Many Guard units were called to service during the COVID-19 pandemic to augment the civil authorities. Regular and Reserve troops can be called up for these functions as well, but there are legal restrictions which must be met. Since Guard units are spread throughout their states and are the best prepared for what is termed Civil Support Operations, they are the first called up in these situations.

Guard units also carry out a purely military role and spend most of their training time on that task. While the National Guard contains large numbers of support units, such as military police and intelligence, virtually all the US Army's reserve combat units are in the National Guard. This includes eight infantry divisions, each with two to four infantry or armoured brigades plus supporting elements. Each division has subordinate units from several different states, as most state's National Guard organisations are not large enough to field an entire division alone.

US Army National Guard Divisions and Brigade Combat Teams	
28th Infantry Division (Pennsylvania)	29th Infantry Division (Virginia)
2nd Infantry Brigade Combat Team (Pennsylvania)	30th Armoured Brigade Combat Team (North Carolina)
56th Stryker Brigade Combat Team (Pennsylvania)	116th Infantry Brigade Combat Team (Virginia)
28th Combat Aviation Brigade (Pennsylvania)	53rd Infantry Brigade Combat Team (Florida)
34th Infantry Division (Minnesota)	35th Infantry Division (Kansas)
1st Armoured Brigade Combat Team (Minnesota)	33rd Infantry Brigade Combat Team (Illinois)
2nd Armoured Brigade Combat Team (Iowa)	39th Infantry Brigade Combat Team (Arkansas)
32nd Infantry Brigade Combat Team (Wisconsin)	45th Infantry Brigade Combat Team (Oklahoma)
116th Cavalry Brigade Combat Team (Idaho)	35th Combat Aviation Brigade (Missouri)
34th Combat Aviation Brigade (Minnesota)	
36th Infantry Division (Texas)	38th Infantry Division (Indiana)
56th Infantry Brigade Combat Team (Texas)	37th Infantry Brigade Combat Team (Ohio)
72nd Infantry Brigade Combat Team (Texas)	76th Infantry Brigade Combat Team (Indiana)
155th Armoured Brigade Combat Team (Mississippi)	278th Armoured Cavalry Regiment (Tennessee)
256th Infantry Brigade Combat Team (Louisiana)	38th Combat Aviation Brigade (Indiana)
36th Combat Aviation Brigade (Texas)	
40th Infantry Division (California)	42nd Infantry Division (New York)
29th Infantry Brigade Combat Team (Hawaii)	27th Infantry Brigade Combat Team (New York)
41st Infantry Brigade Combat Team (Oregon)	44th Infantry Brigade Combat Team (New Jersey)
72nd Infantry Brigade Combat Team (California)	86th Infantry Brigade Combat Team (Vermont)
81st Stryker Brigade Combat Team (Washington)	40th Combat Aviation Brigade (New York)
40th Combat Aviation Brigade (California)	

The National Guard also contains independent brigades and other units including:

16 Manoeuvre Enhancement Brigades - modular units designed to provide support to combat brigades in a variety of missions. They might contain military police, engineer, field artillery, chemical or other units as needed.

8 Field Artillery Brigades – designed to bolster the artillery firepower of a division, corps, or field army. They will include 2 MLRS or HiMARS battalions and additional cannon or rocket artillery battalions as needed.

10 Sustainment Brigades – Provide logistical support to a division, corps, or field army.

3 Military Intelligence Brigades

9 Engineer Brigades

3 Air Defence Artillery Brigades

2 Theatre Tactical Signal Brigades

6 Military Police Brigades

4 Theatre and Combat Aviation Brigades

1 Chemical Brigade

1 Cyber Brigade

1 Missile Defence Brigade

2 Special Forces Groups

Notes: Each division also contains supporting units including field artillery and sustainment (logistics) brigades. Most National Guard brigades draw their heritage from their state's original regiments and maintain that history by using the number of that regiment.

EQUIPMENT

Acquisition and Sustainment

How the army develops, acquires, and maintains war-winning equipment

ABOVE: The M88 recovery vehicle is used to tow broken-down armoured vehicles. It also has a crane used to help change engines and other heavy equipment.
(US ARMY)

Modern warfare requires weapons and equipment of dizzying complexity. Simultaneously, it must be rugged enough to withstand hard use, simple enough for newly trained soldiers to maintain and it needs to remain reliable in different climates, terrain, and weather conditions. This is no simple task, and over time the army has developed an equally complex system to create and maintain the tens of thousands of items which soldiers use.

The process begins when the army realises a need for a new weapon, piece of equipment or something to replace an existing but obsolete item. A programme is created to manage the creative process. This often means engaging with scientists and engineers in national universities and civilian-owned defence contractors, particularly if the new idea requires cutting edge technologies or materials. The army also has its own research and development resources, although in practice these work closely with private industry.

Once the design is finalised, it is usually run through a series of computerised or virtual tests to validate it. Modern computer technology allows much more thorough and speedy development than used to be the case. Eventually a set of prototypes are built for initial assessment at army testing facilities, such as Aberdeen Proving Ground, Maryland, or White Sands Missile Range, New Mexico. Dedicated examiners put the prototypes through trials to determine whether they are viable and what additional refinements they need to be ready for field use.

Eventually the design proceeds to field trials, where regular soldiers put it through everyday use in realistic training exercises. At each stage of development deficiencies are noted and suggestions for improvement made. Once the design is considered ready for general issue, it is standardised and given an official designation. Prototype weapons usually have the letter X in front of the model number; for example, the M1 Abrams tank began development as the XM1. Usually, the numerical designation remains the same.

Weapons, aircraft, and some other items receive 'popular' names according to established conventions. For example, tanks are named after famous generals and helicopters after Native American tribes or chieftains. These conventions are not always followed, however, and some systems simply get a soldier-applied nickname which may not always be favourable, such as the M60 machine gun, known as 'the Pig,' for mixed reasons.

Overall, the acquisition process can take years or even decades in the

LEFT: Army ammunition plants and depots produce and store millions of rounds of ammunition per year, ranging from pistol cartridges to artillery shells. (US ARMY)

case of highly complex equipment. The army does have the Urgent Operational Needs Process, used to rapidly purchase items which fill a gap in current capabilities. During the late 2000s in Iraq, the vulnerability of wheeled vehicles to Improvised Explosive Devices (IEDs) led to the rapid fielding of the Mine Resistant, Ambush Protected (MRAP) series of armoured cars.

A common army adage states, 'Amateurs talk tactics, professionals talk logistics'. A big part of logistics is keeping weapons and equipment operational. Once they are in soldier's hands, they must be maintained. Low level maintenance is conducted by the soldiers who use it, from checking the oil in a vehicle to replacing a broken handset on a radio. Mechanics and technicians in battalion support companies provide the next level of care, performing both maintenance and minor repairs. If the support company can't fix it, the equipment goes to brigade or division level sustainment unit, 'sustainment' being the current term the army uses for its logistics and support units.

If an item is seriously damaged or needs a complete overhaul, it is turned in for depot level maintenance. The army currently operates five major depots around the country, each tasked to support certain types of equipment. For example, artillery systems are sent to the Anniston Army Depot, Alabama. Depots also often upgrade equipment during the overhaul process. Depots also store surplus vehicles, weapons, and equipment.

The army also operates over a dozen arsenals and ammunition plants spread across the Continental United States. Arsenals generally manufacture cannon tubes and barrels, small arms, and similar weapons. Most of these facilities are run by civilian contractors with military oversight.

BELOW: The crew of an M1A2 Abrams perform annual checks on the engine, assisted by mechanics. Armoured vehicles require constant servicing to stay operational. (US ARMY)

EQUIPMENT

M1 Abrams Main Battle Tank

Tried and combat-tested performer

The M1 Abrams is a technological leap forward from the M48 and M-60 Patton-series tanks it replaced. It saw combat service in the Middle East during both the 1991 Gulf War and Operation Iraqi Freedom, as well as active service in Bosnia and Kosovo from 1995-2002.

After the Vietnam conflict, the US Army realised it had fallen behind in the conventional arms race between NATO and the Warsaw pact. It needed a tank which could defeat the latest Soviet designs, such as the T64 and T72. The project began in 1973 with the tank entering service in 1982. Since then, it remains viable due to a continuous series of upgrades.

The latest iteration of the Abrams is M1A2 System Enhancement Package Version 3, or SEPv3, and is currently in production. It uses the 120mm smoothbore main gun, improved armour protection, a counter-Improvised Explosive Device package and other enhancements such as a new auxiliary power unit to run the tank's electronics while the engine is shut down.

The Abrams first saw combat during the 1991 Gulf War, where none were lost to enemy fire, though several were lost to friendly fire and two disabled tanks were destroyed to prevent their capture. The M1 easily the variety

of Soviet-era tanks the Iraqi Army possessed. When the United States returned to Iraq in 2003, the Abrams again made quick work of Iraqi armour but faced a new threat from improvised explosive devices (IEDs). Some were lost to such weapons, but the tank was still vital in supporting infantry during urban fighting.

No US Army M1s saw use in Afghanistan, though the US Marine Corps deployed a company of them in Helmand and Kandahar Provinces from 2010 to 2013. Abrams-equipped units currently deploy to the Baltic states as part of NATO forward presence battlegroup rotations. The Abram's firepower and armour protection make it an effective deterrent against perceived Russian threats toward Eastern European NATO members.

M1 Abrams MBT	
In Service:	1982 – present
Used by:	US Army, US Marine Corps, Australia, Iraq, Egypt, Kuwait, Morocco, Saudi Arabia
Manufacturer:	General Dynamics Land Systems
Unit Cost	$12.5 million in 2020 dollars (£10,192,017)
Produced	1980 – present
Number built:	Approximately 10,000
Specifications	
Mass:	73.6 tons combat weight, M-1A2 SEPv3
Length:	9.77m (32ft)
Width:	3.7m (12ft 1in)
Height:	2.4m (7ft 10in)
Crew:	Four (commander, gunner, loader, driver)
Main Armament:	M256 120mm smoothbore cannon
Secondary Armament:	1 .50 calibre M2HB machine gun at commander's hatch or in a remotely operated station, 1 coaxial M240 7.62mm machine gun, 1 M240 7.62mm machine gun at loader's hatch
Engine:	Honeywell AGT1500 Gas Turbine
Operational Range:	425km (264 miles)
Maximum Speed:	42mph on roads, 30mph cross country

BELOW LEFT: The National Training Center at Fort Irwin, California allows armoured brigades to manoeuvre and train as they would in action. (US ARMY)

BELOW RIGHT: An M1A2 tank negotiates a live fire qualification course. Such courses test the tank crew's skills at movement, target identification and gunnery. (US ARMY)

LEFT: US and Albanian troops take advantage of the Abram's hot engine exhaust to warm their hands after an exercise in Grafenwoehr, Germany. (US ARMY)

EQUIPMENT

M2 Bradley

Infantry Fighting Vehicle

RIGHT: The latest M2A4 Bradley has various electronic and automotive improvements. This will be the main infantry vehicle of the armoured brigade combat teams. (US ARMY)

American mechanised infantrymen have used the M-2 Bradley as their primary infantry fighting vehicle since 1983. The vehicle is reliable and well armoured, carries impressive firepower and has proven easily upgradeable over the past four decades.

Prior American infantry vehicles served as 'battle taxis', transporting soldiers to the battlefield but lacking the armament and protection to endure heavy combat. The Bradley's 25mm Bushmaster cannon and TOW antitank missile launcher gives it the ability to support the six infantrymen the vehicle carries. The M-3 Cavalry Fighting Vehicle variant, intended for reconnaissance troops, carries only two soldiers beyond the three-person crew, but has much more ammunition stowage. Further variants include command post, air defence, engineer,

BELOW: This Bradley's twin launcher box for the TOW missile is in the raised firing position, though the gunner is using the vehicle's coaxial machine gun. (US ARMY)

US ARMY YEARBOOK 2023

M2 Bradley	
In Service:	1981 - present
Used by:	Lebanon, Saudi Arabia, United States
Manufacturer:	BAE Systems
Unit Cost	$4.35 million in 2022 dollars (£3,724,448)
Produced	1981 - present
Number built:	6,724
Specifications	5.25 m (17 ft 3 in)
Mass:	27.6 tons
Length:	6.55m (21ft 6in)
Width:	3.6m (11ft 10in)
Height:	2.98m (9ft 9in)
Crew:	Three (Driver, Gunner, Commander)
Main Armament:	25mm M242 Bushmaster chain gun, twin launcher for BGM71 TOW missile
Secondary Armament:	One coaxial 7.62mm M240 machine gun
Engine:	Cummins VTA-903T diesel
Operational Range:	328km (204 miles)
Maximum Speed:	50kph (31mph)

and artillery forward observer vehicles.

The Bradley first saw combat in the 1991 Gulf War. It has since seen action in the Balkans during the 1990s, the Iraq War and most recently in Syria during the fight against so-called Islamic State (IS). Some have been lost to enemy fire and improvised explosive devices (IEDs), but armour upgrades allow it to stay effective on the battlefield. From 2015 Bradley-equipped units trained with Ukrainian armed forces in Germany and with other NATO allies in Poland, Romania, and the Baltic states.

The latest variant to enter service is the M-2A4, offering upgraded suspension, a larger engine and transmission, and a new electrical system to compensate for the armour and electronics improvements made during the last 20 years. A new fire suppression system and IED jammer are also included.

The US Army is also experimenting with 'optionally manned', robotic versions of the Bradley for future battlefields. This programme is in its early stages, however, and with no other replacement scheduled, the Bradley will likely remain in service for the foreseeable future, equipping the US Army's armoured brigade combat teams.

TOP: Soldiers restock a Bradley with ammunition in Syria, February 2022. The vehicles provide security for forces fighting the so-called Islamic State (IS). (US ARMY)

BELOW: A convoy of Bradleys crosses open desert at the National Training Centre, California. (US ARMY)

EQUIPMENT

Stryker Armoured Vehicle

Wheeled Infantry Carrier

RIGHT: The air defence version of the Stryker carries a four-round pod of Stinger missiles and a rack for two Hellfire missiles. It can also be equipped with a 30mm cannon. (US ARMY)

The Stryker family of wheeled armoured vehicles is now in its third decade of service. Strykers were originally developed during the 1990s to answer a need for an infantry carrier lighter and more easily transported than the M2 Bradley, but better protected and capable than trucks or HMMWVs. The vehicle derives from a Canadian design and is named after two Medal of Honor recipients, one from World War Two and the other from the Vietnam conflict.

Strykers equip eight infantry brigades in the Regular Army and National Guard, filling a space between the armoured brigades and the light infantry brigades. The Stryker is air portable via C130 or larger aircraft. The infantry carrier

BELOW: Two Stryker M1132 engineer squad vehicles cross a bridge over an anti-tank ditch during an exercise. (US ARMY)

US ARMY YEARBOOK 2023

TOP: The basic Stryker is an infantry carrier with a remote weapons station to support the squad it carries. The vehicle has an armour package to provide protection against small arms fire up to 14.5mm and artillery shrapnel (US ARMY)

Stryker	
In Service:	2002 - present
Used by:	United States
Manufacturer:	General Dynamics Land Systems
Unit Cost	$5,000,000 (£4,361,075)
Produced	2001 - present
Number built:	4,900
Specifications	5.25 m (17 ft 3 in)
Mass:	16.47 tons
Length:	6.95m (22ft 10in)
Width:	2.72m (8ft 11in)
Height:	2.64m (8ft 8in)
Crew:	Two (Driver, Commander) plus nine troops in the infantry carrier
Main Armament:	One .50-calibre machine gun or one 40mm MK19 grenade launcher
Engine:	Caterpillar 3126 (350hp)
Operational Range:	532km (330 miles)
Maximum Speed:	96.5kph (62mph)

uses a remote weapons station which allows the crew to fire safely from within the vehicle.

There are several variants used with a Stryker brigade, easing maintenance issues, and providing for common driver training and tactical employment. Variants include the infantry carrier, air defence vehicle, mortar carrier, fire support vehicle for artillery forward observers, command vehicle, medical evacuation, engineer vehicle, anti-tank missile vehicle, and reconnaissance vehicle. A Mobile Gun System (MGS) variant carried a turret with a 105mm cannon, but this type has been retired due to problems with the cannon autoloader and the inability to upgrade its hull configuration. Many infantry carriers are being retrofitted with a 30mm gun turret for increased effectiveness against enemy armoured vehicles.

Stryker brigades saw combat in Iraq and Afghanistan. While there were concerns about the vehicle's ability to survive IED blasts and hits from Rocket Propelled Grenades (RPGs), troops who used the vehicle were generally positive about it, citing its toughness and reliability. Units installed slat armour to help against RPG attacks. Several Strykers struck by large IEDs suffered damage, but the crews survived, often unharmed. One vehicle was blown onto its side by a 500lb car bomb, but the crew was uninjured, and the vehicle was drivable when rolled upright.

BELOW: The M1129 mortar carrier has a 120mm mortar which can fire precision munitions. This crew prepares to fire during an exercise in Japan. (US NAVY)

www.keymilitary.com 73

EQUIPMENT

Light Armoured Vehicles

Mobile protected vehicles for various roles

RIGHT: The army uses HMMWVs in a wide assortment of roles; this vehicle is modified to resemble a Russian-built BRDM armoured car for opposing force training scenarios. (US ARMY)

BELOW: The M1117 Armored Security Vehicle is an upgraded version of the 1960s-era V150 Commando armoured car. This vehicle carries a .50-calibre machine gun and 40mm MK19 grenade launcher in the turret. (US ARMY)

ABOVE: The M113 series has been in service since the Vietnam conflict in a wide variety of roles, including troop carrier, field ambulance and command post. These are M1064 120mm Mortar Carriers on exercise in Poland. (US ARMY)

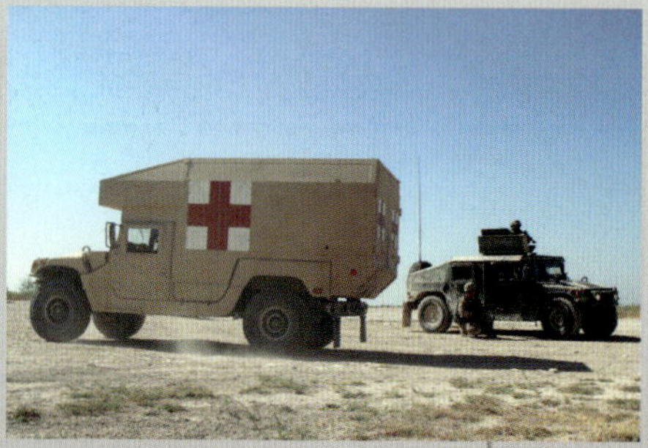

ABOVE: Some 160,000 High Mobility Multipurpose Wheeled Vehicles (HMMWVs) were acquired from the 1980s onwards, replacing the famous Jeep. Here, an M997 ambulance drives past an M1151 up-armoured troop carrier during an exercise at Fort Hood, Texas. (US ARMY)

US ARMY YEARBOOK 2023

LEFT: Oshkosh Corporation's Light All-Terrain Vehicle (L-ATV) provides a comparable level of protection to the MRAP vehicles and is supplementing the HMMWV as a standard light armoured multi-role vehicle. (OSHKOSH DEFENCE)

BELOW: Tens of thousands of Mine Resistant – Ambush Protected (MRAP) vehicles were acquired during the wars in Iraq and Afghanistan. They are generally like those in UK service and have been liberally distributed to allied and coalition nations worldwide. (US ARMY)

EQUIPMENT

M109 Paladin

Self-propelled 155mm howitzer

RIGHT: A Paladin at Hohenfels, Germany during a NATO training exercise. (US ARMY)

M109A6 Paladin	
In Service:	1963 - present
Used by:	Saudi Arabia, United States – older models in service with numerous other nations
Manufacturer:	BAE Systems
Unit Cost	$11.1 million (£9.58 million)
Produced	1963 - present
Number built:	950
Specifications	
Mass:	34.25 tons
Length:	9.1m (29ft 10in)
Width:	3.15m (10ft 4in)
Height:	3.25m (10ft 8in)
Crew:	Four (Driver, Gunner, Loader, Section Chief/ Commander)
Main Armament:	M284 155mm howitzer
Secondary Armament:	One roof-mounted .50-calibre M2HB machine gun
Engine:	Detroit Diesel 8V71T (440hp)
Operational Range:	290km (180 miles)
Maximum Speed:	56kph (35mph)

The M109 series of self-propelled (SP) howitzers is in its seventh decade of service in the US Army. The current M109A6 added the name Paladin to the vehicle and took advantage of the electronics revolution by incorporating a digital fire control system, allowing the crew to hook into the artillery fire control network. This enables fast gun-laying and firing, usually followed by a fast movement from the firing point to avoid counterbattery fire. Paladins can receive fire missions while on the move, stop and then fire within 30 seconds. The Paladin is lightly armoured to protect the crew from artillery shrapnel and small arms fire.

The first M109s saw action in the Vietnam conflict and in every US-involved conflict since. It is in service with numerous other nations and was made under license in South Korea. A small number were refurbished in the UK and subsequently transferred to Ukraine.

An upgraded model, the M109A7, is beginning to enter service in small numbers. This version incorporates drivetrain and electrical upgrades. M109s are accompanied by the M992 series of ammunition carriers, built on the same hull.

BELOW: A Paladin fires a high-angle mission while its M992 ammunition carrier stands by to replenish 155mm shells and powder charges. (US ARMY)

M777 155mm Howitzer

Lightweight field gun

M777 155mm Howitzer	
In Service:	2005 to present
Used by:	Australia, Canada, India. Saudi Arabia, United States, Ukraine
Manufacturer:	BAE Systems
Produced:	2000 to present
Number Built	1,300 to present; also license-built in India
Specifications	
Mass:	4,200kg (9,300lb)
Length:	10.7m (35ft) when deployed for firing
Crew	Five to eight personnel
Rate of fire:	Two rounds per minute (sustained) / Five rounds per minute (maximum)
Maximum barrel elevation	71.2°
Maximum firing range	22.5km (14 miles) standard; 30km (19 miles) using rocket assisted projectile (RAP); 40 km (25 miles) using Excalibur guided round

The heavy firepower of non-armoured brigade combat teams (BCTs) comes from the M777 howitzer. Each infantry BCT has a battery of these 155mm howitzers for fire support; Stryker Brigades have a battalion composed of three batteries of the 'Triple 7'. Many corps-level artillery brigades have a battalion of these hard-hitting cannon assigned to them.

The gun is manufactured by its developer, the UK-based BAE Systems. Initially designated the Ultralight Field Howitzer (UFH), since its adoption by the US military, BAE has spread production to its American subsidiary. Light weight remained an important feature of the weapon and the use of titanium in its construction makes it easier to transport and emplace.

The M777 first saw combat in 2008 in Iraq and Afghanistan, where its long range, accuracy, and ability to be quickly set up for action was appreciated by soldiers. The weapon saw further service in the Middle East during the campaign against the so-called Islamic State (IS), providing both precision and counter-battery fire using the M982 Excalibur guided artillery round, often striking within 4m of their target.

TOP: A M777 sling-loaded by a CH47 Chinook heavy lift helicopter during NATO training exercise Sabre Strike in Poland. (US ARMY)

BELOW: Soldiers of the 101st Airborne Division fire a night mission against so-called Islamic State (IS) forces near Mosul, Iraq in 2016. American artillery provided extensive support to Iraqi forces. (US ARMY)

EQUIPMENT

M119A3 105mm Howitzer

A venerable light artillery piece

RIGHT: The digital fire control system enables the M119 to use precision munitions and GPS navigation which allows soldiers to fire within two to three minutes, rather than 10 minutes with previous equipment. (US ARMY)

M119A3 105mm Howitzer	
In Service:	1989 to present
Used by:	Bahrain, Benin, Bosnia-Herzegovina, Botswana, Brazil, Ireland, Kenya, Malawi, Morocco, Nepal, New Zealand, Oman, Portugal, Spain, Thailand, Turkey, United Arab Emirates, United Kingdom, United States
Manufacturer:	Rock Island Arsenal, Illinois
Produced:	1989 to present
Number Built	1,000 in US
Specifications	
Mass:	1,936kg
Length:	8.8m (28ft 10in)
Width:	1.78m (5ft 10in)
Height:	1.37m (4ft 6in)
Crew	Five to seven personnel
Rate of fire:	Three rounds per minute (sustained)
Maximum firing range	17,500m (19,138yd)/19,500m (21,325yd) using rocket assisted projectile (RAP)

The venerable but still effective M119A3 howitzer equips the artillery battalions of light infantry, air assault and airborne divisions and their subordinate brigade combat teams. This lightweight 105mm cannon is in service with both regular army and National Guard artillery units. It is a license-built version of the British L119 light gun, in American service since 1989.

US troops first used the M119 in combat during Operation Desert Storm in 1991. Since then, it has seen service in Iraq and Afghanistan. The weapon can be transported by helicopter or towed by light wheeled vehicles including the HMMWV. It can also be dropped by parachute. In over three decades of service the '105' has proven to be a reliable and accurate weapon, with no firm plans to replace it.

The latest version of the weapon, the M119A3, includes improvement to the recoil system, a digital fire control system and a navigation system. The upgrade also allows the weapon to operate in temperatures down to minus 46ºC (-51ºF). It can fire the entire range of NATO standard ammunition, including high explosive, illumination, smoke, and rocket-assisted extended range rounds.

BELOW: Soldiers of the 173rd Airborne Brigade fire their howitzer in direct fire mode. Shooting directly at a target is usually a desperation tactic for field artillery units. (US ARMY)

US ARMY YEARBOOK 2023

M270 Multiple Launch Rocket System

Steel Rain

M270A2 Multiple Launch Rocket System	
In service:	1983 to present
Used by:	Bahrain, Egypt, Finland, Greece, France, Germany, Israel, Italy, Japan, Saudi Arabia, South Korea, Turkey, Ukraine, United Kingdom, United States
Manufacturer:	Lockheed Martin
Produced:	1982 to 2003; production of improved models using existing vehicles continues
Number built:	1,300 with 385 in US service
Specifications:	
Mass:	25,000kg (55,100lb)
Length:	6.85m (22ft 6in)
Width:	2.97m (9ft 9in)
Height:	2.59m (8ft 6in)
Crew:	Three (Commander, Gunner, Driver)
Armament:	Two rocket pods with six 227mm rockets each or two missile pods with one missile each
Engine:	Cummins Diesel Engine with 600hp in M270A2
Operational range:	480km (298 miles)
Maximum speed:	64kph (40mph) on roads

TOP: Vehicle commanders generally guide their launchers by standing in its top hatch to allow a better view of the area around the vehicle.
(US ARMY)

MIDDLE: The M28A2 Reduced Range Practice Rocket (RRPR), nicknamed the 'Ripper', has a shorter range of only 9km, allowing units to practice firing at smaller military bases.
(US ARMY)

The M270 entered combat in 1991 during Operation Desert Storm. Batteries equipped with the MLRS poured a steady deluge of rockets and missiles on the Iraqi army, destroying fighting positions, vehicles, logistics depots and headquarters units.

When Allied infantry and armour finally moved in, Iraqi soldiers surrendered by the thousands. Many of them paid a grim testament to the effectiveness of the M270 when they begged: "No more steel rain."

The US Army created the MLRS in the aftermath of the Vietnam conflict, when it realised the Soviets had used American distraction to field new artillery systems. The US Army needed something to even the odds, and the resulting M270 entered service in 1983. Developed jointly with the United Kingdom, France and West Germany, the new launcher provided a leap forward in mass firepower.

Today the original cluster bomb-style munitions have been replaced with unitary warheads using precision guidance in both standard rockets and the larger ATACMS missiles. Like most of the army's legacy weapons, the M270 has been steadily upgraded with improved electronics and hydraulic systems to enable the weapon to fire and move quickly to avoid counterbattery fire.

After the Gulf War, MLRS has been deployed to Iraq and Afghanistan. The system equips numerous Active Duty and National Guard artillery battalions.

BOTTOM: Firing a rocket creates a very visible launch signature; the launcher must move very quickly afterward to avoid counterbattery fire.
(US ARMY)

www.keymilitary.com

EQUIPMENT

M142 HiMARS

Wheeled Rocket and Missile Launcher

RIGHT: A HiMARS launcher disembarks from a C-17 transport during an emergency readiness exercise. The system can fire within minutes of leaving the aircraft. (US ARMY)

M142 High Mobility Artillery Rocket System	
In service:	2010 to present
Used by:	Jordan, Romania, Singapore, Ukraine, United Arab Emirates, United States Army, and Marine Corps, with pending sales to Australia, Estonia, Poland and Taiwan
Manufacturer:	Lockheed Martin
Produced:	2005 to present
Number built:	At least 528, with over 363 in US Army service as procurement continues
Specifications	
Mass:	16,239kg (35,800lb)
Length:	7m (23ft)
Width:	2.4m (7ft 10in)
Height:	3.2m (10ft 6in)
Crew:	Three (Commander, Gunner, Driver)
Armament:	One rocket pod with six 227mm rockets or one missile pod with one missile each
Engine:	Caterpillar Diesel Engine with 290hp in M270A2
Operational range:	483km (300 miles)
Maximum speed:	94kph (58mph) on roads

The M142 High Mobility Artillery Rocket System (HiMARS) is a lighter version of the M270 MLRS. The vehicle is a variant of the standard five-ton Medium Tactical Vehicle truck mounting a launch system for a single pod holding either six rockets or a single Advanced Tactical Missile System (ATACMS) long range missile. HiMARS can use any of the MLRS family of munitions including guided and unguided rockets out to a range of over 70 kilometres. It will also be able to fire the new Precision Strike Missile scheduled to enter service in 2024.

HiMARS entered service in 2005 and has quickly become the artillery weapon of choice for long range precision strikes. As a wheeled vehicle it is much lighter than the tracked MLRS and can be air transported by a C-130 cargo aircraft. HiMARS is also capable of precision fire as close as 200 metres from friendly troops, targeting command posts, enemy artillery positions and logistics targets such as ammunition dumps and troop assembly areas.

The first combat deployment for HiMARs came in 2010 in Afghanistan, and it has seen service in Iraq and Syria against both the so-called Islamic State (IS) and pro-government Syrian forces. During the 2018 Battle of Khasham in Syria, US HiMARS fired rockets against pro-government Syrian forces led by Russian private military contractors, inflicting heavy casualties.

HiMARS is in service with 17 Regular and National Guard field artillery battalions in the US Army. The system is still in production as the army acquires more to bolster its artillery firepower. Several nations have purchased or expressed interest in it, guaranteeing further production. At least 16 have been provided to Ukrainian forces during the current Russian invasion, with training provided by US Army soldiers in Germany.

BELOW: HiMARS launchers from the Colorado National Guard 3/157th Field Artillery live fire their launchers at Kuwait's Udairi range, June 2022. (US ARMY)

Air Defence Artillery

Protection from aerial threats, drones to ballistic missiles

During the wars in Iraq and Afghanistan US Army air defence units took second place since the enemy lacked any sort of air power. As the nation's military awoke to the threat posed by peer actors such as Russia and China, the army realised the degree to which these vital capabilities had atrophied. Air defence units are now training to act on a battlefield with a sky full of enemy planes.

The Air Defence Artillery branch fields five major weapons systems. The first is the AN/TWQ1 Avenger, a HMMWV truck modified to carry a turret mounting a .50-calibre machine gun and two four-round missile pods for the Stinger infrared homing missile. The system has been in service since 1989 and is now mostly used by National Guard units.

Manoeuvre Short-Range Air Defence (M-SHORAD) is a Stryker armoured car configured to carry Stinger and Hellfire missiles along with a 30mm cannon and 7.62mm machine gun. They are still entering service and there are plans to field at least four battalions. Supplementing these weapons is C-RAM, the Counter Rocket, Artillery and Mortar system. It is based on the naval Phalanx 20mm gatling gun. Video of a C-RAM shooting down Taliban rockets near Kabul airport went 'viral' in 2021.

The army also operates two large surface to air missile systems. The current MIM104 Patriot is a mobile system effective against aircraft, missiles, and drones, updated from the original model used during the Gulf War in 1991. Terminal High Altitude Area Défense (THAAD) is an anti-ballistic missile system designed to shoot down enemy missiles in their terminal (descent) phase. THAAD batteries are deployed around the world to defend against nations with significant ballistic missile capabilities.

TOP: THAAD is a combat-tested system, reportedly shooting down a Houthi ballistic missile fired at a target in the UAE in 2021. (US MISSILE DEFENSE AGENCY)

MIDDLE: Patriot missiles can be used against aircraft, cruise, or ballistic missiles. This launcher is being inspected after a launch during an exercise in Palau. (US ARMY)

BOTTOM LEFT: M-SHORAD is being fielded first in Europe to bolster NATO air defence capabilities. This crew is firing on a drone during an exercise in Estonia, 2022. (TENNESSEE NG)

BOTTOM RIGHT: The Avenger is the army's legacy short range air defence system, gradually being supplanted by the newer M-SHORAD. (USAF)

EQUIPMENT

AH64 Apache

Attack Helicopter

RIGHT: Apaches still see active service in the Middle East. These aircraft are in Syria giving air support to forces fighting the remnants of the so-called Islamic State. (US ARMY)

BELOW: Aircrew in Poland for NATO exercises. The co-pilot/gunner sits in the forward position with the pilot above and behind. (US ARMY)

BELOW RIGHT: Apaches can land on warships to rearm and refuel. Here two helicopters of the 17th Cavalry perform deck landing qualifications aboard the USS Lewis B. Puller (ESB3). (USMC PHOTO)

AH64 Apache Attack Helicopter	
In service:	1986 - present
Used by:	Egypt, Greece, India, Indonesia, Israel, Japan, Kuwait, Morocco (on order), Netherlands, Qatar, Saudi Arabia, Singapore, South Korea, Taiwan, United Arab Emirates United Kingdom, United States
Manufacturer:	Boeing
Produced:	1984 – present
Number Built:	2,400
Specifications	
Length:	17.7m (58ft 2in)
Rotor diameter:	14.6m (48ft)
Height:	3.9m (12ft 8in)
Maximum take-off weight:	10,433kg (23,000lb)
Crew:	Two (pilot and co-pilot/gunner)
Powerplant:	Two General Electric T700-GE-701 turboshaft engines
Maximum Speed:	293kph (182mph)
Range:	480km (300 miles)
Guns:	One M230 30mm chain gun with 1,200 rounds
Missiles/Rockets:	Up to 16 Hellfire missiles, or 76 2.75in rockets. May also carry Stinger air-to-air missiles, AGM-65 Maverick, or Spike air-to-ground missiles.

The AH64 Apache is the US Army's attack helicopter and has been in service since 1985. Designed as a tank-buster during the Cold War, the design includes heavy armour for the crew, able to withstand up to 23mm cannon fire. Its heavy weapons load is a legacy of its origins as an anti-armour vehicle. The first Apache unit entered service in 1986 and there are currently over 1,200 in army use.

The latest version is the AH64E, which has more powerful engines, upgraded transmission, and stronger landing gear than its predecessor and is fitted with new composite rotor blades. It can also control unmanned aerial vehicles (UAVs). Like most of the latest army weapons systems, the AH64E can link with other air and ground platforms through a digital information system.

Apaches have logged over 4.8m flight hours in American service, with over 1.3m hours in combat. This includes the Gulf War, the Balkans, Iraq, and Afghanistan. While a few have been lost to accidents or hostile fire, most Apaches suffering damage are able to return safely due to their tough design.

In Iraq, ground troops noticed insurgents often retreated or abandoned their plans when Apache helicopters were spotted flying overhead. Army Apaches have flown from aircraft carriers and other warships.

The Apache will remain the army's sole attack helicopter until at least the 2030s. They are regularly deployed to the Middle East and as part of American contributions to NATO forward battlegroups.

UH60 Blackhawk

Multirole Helicopter

UH60 Blackhawk	
In service:	1979-present
Used by:	Albania, Australia, Austria, Bahrain, Brazil, Brunei, Chile, People's Republic of China, Colombia, Croatia, Egypt, Israel, Japan, Jordan, Lithuania, Malaysia, Mexico, Morocco, Philippines, Poland, Portugal, Saudi Arabia, South Korea, Slovakia, Sweden, Taiwan, Thailand, Tunisia, Turkey, United Arab Emirates, United States
Manufacturer:	Sikorsky Aircraft, a division of Lockheed Martin
Produced:	1978-present
Number Built:	Over 4,000
Specifications:	
Length:	19.8m (64ft 10in)
Rotor diameter:	16.4m (53ft 8in)
Height:	5.1m (16ft 10in)
Maximum take-off weight:	9,979kg (22,000lb)
Crew:	Four (Two pilots and two crew chiefs/gunners)
Powerplant:	Two General Electric T700-GE-701C/D turboshaft engines
Maximum Speed:	294kph (183mph)
Range:	590km (370 miles)
Armament	64kph (40mph) on roads
Guns:	Two 7.62mm or 12.7mm machine guns
Missiles/Rockets:	Can be fitted with hardpoints for a combination of Hellfire or Stinger missiles, and 2.75in rockets

TOP: Two New Jersey National Guard helicopters practicing air assault insertion techniques. This allows the crew to land a fully armed infantry squad in just a few seconds. (US ARMY)

The Blackhawk has become as ubiquitous as the legendary Vietnam-era UH1 'Huey' it replaced. The aircraft has proven as durable, reliable, and versatile as the Huey, filling multiple roles including transport, medical evacuation, command and control, cargo, search and rescue and special operations. The builder, Sikorsky, has a long history of proven rotary-wing designs.

Design and testing of the Blackhawk began in the 1970s, with aircraft entering service in 1979. Since then, it has served in every American conflict including Grenada, Panama, the Gulf War, the Balkans, Iraq, Afghanistan, and Syria. While the AH64 Apache is preferred for attack missions, the Blackhawk can be fitted with external hardpoints to carry the same weapons or auxiliary fuel tanks to extend their operating range. In can also carry an 11-soldier infantry squad or up to 4,082kg (9,000lb) of external cargo.

The design is so successful it flies or has flown with some 30 nations. Interestingly, the People's Republic of China even has a few dozen, having bought them in the 1980s before Sino-American relations soured. The US Navy, Coast Guard and Air Force also fly them.

UH60s are the backbone of US Army Combat Aviation Brigades and are expected to continue flying for years to come, as the new Bell V280 Valor completes testing and enters service. Both active and reserve component units fly the Blackhawk; at this point the children of the design's original pilots are now flying them across the globe.

BOTTOM: A Blackhawk crew prepares for a flight demonstration of a new degraded vision piloting system which allows the pilots to fly safely during conditions, of darkness, fog, or dust. (US ARMY)

EQUIPMENT

Unmanned Aerial Vehicles

UAVs are among the major new systems for future conflicts

RIGHT: The RQ11 Raven is a company-level UAV small enough to be launched by a soldier simply throwing it into the air. It weighs less than 2kg and can fly for 1.5 hours. It carries colour and night vision cameras. (US ARMY)

BELOW: The RQ7B Shadow drone is used at the brigade level for reconnaissance, surveillance, and target acquisition. The latest versions have six to nine hours endurance and a cruising speed of 130kph (81mph). (US ARMY)

Unmanned Aerial Vehicles are among the biggest threats on future battlefields. They have figured prominently in every major conflict since the Gulf War in 1991 and early versions saw use in the 1960s. Initially limited to observation and reconnaissance roles, drones are now often armed, and some are weapons themselves.

In the US Army, UAVs see use down to the company level. The service has several thousand on the inventory, ranging from the small RQ11, light enough to be launched by hand, to the large RQ7B Shadow, widely used for scouting and targeting missions ranging from artillery to air strikes.

The larger MQ1C Gray Eagle also fills typical reconnaissance and

US ARMY YEARBOOK 2023

ABOVE: The MQ1C Gray Eagle provides target identification and battle damage assessment of targets. They can also carry four Hellfire missiles. (US ARMY)

ABOVE: A swarm of UAVs flies over a mock village at the National Training Centre in California. Large army training events now routinely include attacks by drone swarms, hinting at future expectations. (US ARMY)

targeting roles but can also carry four Hellfire missiles for ground attack or eight Stinger air-to air missiles for anti-helicopter/aircraft missions.

The best-known UAV in army service is actually classified as a missile. The Switchblade 300 weighs only 2.5kg (5.5lb) and has a warhead as powerful as a 40mm grenade; detonation fires a directional spray of pellets like a shotgun. Range is up to 10km (6.2 miles) using a small electric engine so quiet targets rarely detect its approach before it strikes. Soldiers use a small Ground Control Station (GCS) to guide the Switchblade. It can be used against ground targets or other drones. The larger Switchblade 600 is designed to attack armoured vehicles with a warhead based on the Javelin missile. Switchblades became famous when the United States provided them to the Ukrainian military during the Russian invasion in 2022, where they were used with deadly effect. The UK also operates the Switchblade.

TOP: Defence against commercially made drones is a relatively new yet important skill for soldiers. Here, US and Indian soldiers train on anti-drone devices in Alaska. (US ARMY)

www.keymilitary.com

EQUIPMENT

Engineer Equipment

Construction, demolition, mine clearing, and bridging

RIGHT: The Husky Vehicle-Mounted Mine Detection vehicle carries a ground penetrating radar system capable of detecting anti-tank mines and Improvised Explosive Devices (IEDs). The Husky saw extensive use in Afghanistan. (US ARMY)

BELOW: The TALON robot is used for investigating and eliminating threats from bombs, mines and other explosive devices. Here, an engineer is remotely controlling the robot during a certification course, using it to place an object in a box. (US ARMY)

BOTTOM: The M1ABV (Assault Breacher Vehicle) is equipped as an earth mover, mine clearance vehicle and demolitions vehicle. It moves with infantry and armour to clear a path through obstacles such as ditches, minefields or blocked roads. It is based on the M1 Abrams chassis. (US ARMY)

ABOVE: An M9 Armoured Combat Earthmover (ACE) creates a breach in an anti-tank ditch during training in the California desert. The ACE is used for breaching obstacles and digging fighting positions for vehicles. It is essentially a heavily armoured bulldozer. (US ARMY RESERVE)

US ARMY YEARBOOK 2023

BELOW: The M1074 Joint Assault Bridge can lay its bridge across an 18-metre gap in three minutes. It is equipped with smoke grenade launchers to obscure its position during combat crossing missions. (US ARMY)

ABOVE: Engineer boats are used to brace a section of the Improved Ribbon bridge (IRB) while it is emplaced during a training event on the Arkansas River. River crossings are hazardous operations and require extensive planning and support to successfully complete. (US ARMY RESERVE)

ABOVE: Combat engineers assemble a Bangalore torpedo to destroy a concertina wire obstacle during a live fire training exercise. The Bangalore has been in use since World War Two. (IDAHO NG)

ABOVE: The Buffalo mine clearance vehicle has a 30ft-long robotic arm used to investigate and deal with mines and explosive devices. The vehicle's high ground clearance allows any explosions under it to dissipate, reducing their effect. (US ARMY)

ABOVE: The Explosive Hazard Pre-Detonation Roller (EHP Roller) attaches to the front of mine protected vehicles to detonate mines and IEDs ahead of the vehicle. They are used to make roads safe for other vehicles to transit. (US ARMY)

www.keymilitary.com

EQUIPMENT

Logistics Vehicles

Delivering food, ammunition, and fuel

RIGHT: For arctic and snowy terrain, the army relies upon the venerable Small Unit Support Vehicle (SUSV) to carry troops and supplies. The new 11th Airborne Division will use these vehicles until the new Cold Weather All-Terrain vehicle enters service. (US ARMY)

RIGHT: The Heavy Expanded Mobility Tactical Truck (HEMTT) family of vehicles has been in service since 1982 and includes cargo, recovery, and tanker variants, among others. It also has its own series of trailers. (US ARMY)

ABOVE: Heavy Equipment Transporter trucks, known as 'HETs', can haul any of the Army's armoured vehicles. This saves wear on expensive tracked vehicles and avoids damage to roads. An improved version now entering service can carry up to 90 tons. (US ARMY)

ABOVE: The army's standard supply haulers are in the Family of Medium Tactical Vehicles (FMTV). Like most Army wheeled vehicles they can be upgraded with armour kits for better survivability. (US ARMY)

US ARMY YEARBOOK 2023

Uniforms

The clothing, armour, and equipment a soldier needs

ABOVE: A Staff Sergeant dons his Joint Service Lightweight Integrated Suit Technology (JSLIST) chemical protective gear during an exercise. Soldiers will put on their M50 gas mask first, followed by the suit, gloves and over boots. Afterward they will place their helmet and equipment over the suit. (US ARMY)

LEFT: This infantry soldier's body armour is adorned with the equipment he must have during this patrol in Syria: spare ammunition, a first aid kit, light sticks, and a Camelbak hydration pack on his back. (US ARMY)

BELOW: The Soldier Protection System intends to provide superior ballistic protection to troops while reducing weight. This 60mm mortar crew is wearing the Integrated Head Protection System (IHPS) helmet and the Modular Scalable Vest (MSV) over their combat uniforms. These items have entered service in the last two years and benefit from years of experience in recent conflicts. (US ARMY)

ABOVE: This soldier has night vision goggles attached to his helmet, a Net Warrior command and control system clipped to his chest, and a medical kit with a tourniquet (wrapped in red tape) at his waist. His rifle has a Family of Weapon Sights – Individual (FWS-I), which transmits an aiming reticule to his goggles, allowing him to aim and fire accurately even around corners. (US ARMY)

ABOVE: The Army has recently chosen a new dress uniform, practically identical to those worn during World War Two. Known as the Army Green Service Uniform, they are nicknamed 'pinks and greens' due to the pinkish hue of the trousers. (US ARMY)

EQUIPMENT

Small Arms

Rifles, machine guns, mortars and more

RIGHT: The M136 AT-4 is a lightweight, portable anti-armour rocket used by numerous armies worldwide. Over 600,000 have been produced, and the designation AT4 is a play on the rocket's 84mm diameter. It is light enough for infantry soldiers to carry one in addition to their basic load. (US ARMY)

ABOVE: The M240B is a licence-produced version of the FN MAG machine gun, known in the UK as the L7 GPMG. It is a reliable, robust weapon which can be fitted with a variety of optical, thermal, and night-vision sights to improve target engagement. (US ARMY)

ABOVE: The 9mm M17 pistol, made by SIG-Sauer, is gradually replacing the Beretta M9 as the army's primary sidearm. The weapon has a modular design, with variable grip sizes to better fit different soldier's hand sizes. (US ARMY)

BELOW: The M249 Squad Automatic Weapon (SAW) is a belt-fed 5.56mm light machine gun, a license-produced version of the Belgian-designed Minimi. It can engage targets out to 800 metres, at a cyclic rate of 700-850 rounds per minute. It does suffer from the same lack of penetration of body armour as the M4, and so is being replaced with the M250, firing a more powerful 6.8mm cartridge. (US ARMY)

US ARMY YEARBOOK 2023

FAR LEFT: Officially designated as an Anti-Material Sniper Rifle, the M107 fires the same round as the .50-calibre machine gun, with an effective range of 1,800 metres. Snipers have made wide use of the weapon in Iraq and Afghanistan. The weapon's large muzzle brake helps to reduce the heavy recoil. (US ARMY)

LEFT: A derivative of the M16 rifle, the more compact M4 Carbine serves as the army's standard rifle, firing a 5.56mm NATO cartridge. It is light and simple to operate, but lacks penetrating power against modern body armour, so it is now being replaced by the new, larger-calibre M5. (US ARMY)

LEFT: The FGM-148 Javelin missile is the army's primary anti-tank missile system. It is a fire-and-forget system using infrared guidance, allowing operators to take cover immediately after firing. It can operate in top attack mode, striking an armoured vehicle through its thinner roof armour. (US ARMY)

BELOW: Mortars are the infantry's own artillery, with the army issuing weapons in 60, 81 and 120mm calibres. This M252A1 81mm mortar, shown here firing blue training rounds, has a range of 5,935 metres and can fire up to 30 rounds per minute. (US ARMY)

www.keymilitary.com

EQUIPMENT

Communications Equipment

A key to dispersed operations in the 21st century

ABOVE: 'Filling' a radio means loading the latest encryption information into it to prevent enemy eavesdropping. Knowing how to do so is one of the basic tasks of soldiering in the 21st century. (US ARMY)

ABOVE: Satellite dishes now rank among the most common items seen at headquarters' units. The army uses modular designs for rapid assembly and movement. (US ARMY)

ABOVE: The Single Channel Ground and Airborne Radio System (SINCGARS) radio is the US Army's standard field radio. It uses encryption and frequency hopping to prevent enemy interception of transmissions. Here, two NCOs use one to communicate with a C17 cargo aircraft approaching their drop zone. (US ARMY RESERVE)

ABOVE: The Satellite Transportable Terminal (STT) enables over the horizon communications for field units. It can be set up in as little as 15 minutes and carries its own power supply for quick use. It can deliver voice, video, and data communications. (US ARMY)

Future Wars, Future Weapons

Warfare will be faster, more lethal, and more automated

LEFT: Allies are critically important to the US Army. Maj Gen James Bowder, Director of Futures, Army Command UK, signs a cooperative agreement with US Maj Gen Walter Rugen to study future cooperation on helicopter programs. (US ARMY)

Preparing for the wars of the future is a complicated and risky undertaking. The pace of technological change in the 21st century means ideas, plans and equipment can be rendered obsolete within a few years, often before they are even fully realised or fielded. Planning ahead is still vital; forward-thinking military organisations must resist the tendency to 'fight the last war'. Instead, the US Army is readying itself to face a wide range of threats with limited information on their exact nature.

The army spent decades fighting wars against insurgents who could inflict casualties but were never an existential threat to the United States. Recent and future efforts are focusing on wars with what are called peer and near-peer adversaries; namely, Russia and China, with Iran as a third possible opponent.

China, Iran, and North Korea are developing Anti-Access/Area Denial (A2AD) networks, seeking to keep the US away from both their own territories and those they wish to conquer. Neutralising these networks are a major focus of the US military's future planning.

There are many facets to the future fight as it is currently envisaged. The army will need more long-range capabilities in artillery, rockets, and missiles along with improved air defences. Units will disperse over wider areas to avoid becoming easy targets, but it will be difficult to hide from an enemy with modern reconnaissance abilities. Advanced sensors are needed to find the enemy before they find you; 'locate first, fire first, hit first' is the future soldier's mantra. Automated and robotic systems will become ever more common.

For the US Army, the most important component of future conflict are allies. The army will not fight a future conflict alone. There are many existing and long-established relationships, such as the US membership of NATO and the 'Special Relationship' that the US enjoys with the United Kingdom, which effectively extends to Canada, Australia, and New Zealand as well. Other long-standing coalitions include those with Japan and South Korea, but many other local partnerships exist.

American soldiers frequently train with their counterparts from allied and aligned nations for mutual understanding of their respective tactics, organisation, and capabilities. During wartime, such understanding is invaluable and can mean the difference between victory or defeat.

BELOW: Robotic Systems figure prominently in future US Army war planning; numerous systems are under study. (US ARMY)

FUTURE WARS, FUTURE WEAPONS

Pivot to the Pacific

Increased focus on the Indo-Pacific

RIGHT: American and Filipino infantrymen cross a creek during a jungle operations course at the annual Salaknib exercise in the Philippines. (US ARMY)

The 'Pivot to the Pacific' is a term used to describe the United States government's increased focus on the political and military situation in the Indo-Pacific region. How successful or dedicated this effort has been at the civil government's level has been the subject of extensive debate for years. The US Army, however, is cognizant of the threat of future conflicts in the region and is preparing to operate throughout the area.

The Indo-Pacific is a vast region with widely varying terrain, from the jungles of the various Pacific islands to the frigid mountains of the Korean peninsula and the Himalayas. The two major potential adversaries in this region are North Korea and China; a sizable Russian presence is also a concern. A Chinese invasion of Taiwan is generally seen as the most likely scenario for a war with China. Operations involving North Korea could mean a range of events from a North Korean attack on South

BELOW: American, South Korean, and Japanese junior officers take part in an exchange symposium at Camp Humphreys, South Korea. The three nations coordinate on defence issues concerning North Korea and, increasingly, China. (US ARMY)

Korea or Japan to a collapse of the North Korean regime requiring a humanitarian intervention.

The vast distances and oceans of the region cause many planners and pundits to assume a war here would be a naval and air fight with little need for ground troops, beyond perhaps the US Marine Corps, famous for its Pacific operations in World War Two. However, while the Marine Corps is highly skilled, it is not large enough to fight a major war. It is also a little-known fact that the US Army made more, and larger, amphibious assaults during World War Two than the Marines due to its greater size, although the Marines did invent amphibious tactics. While amphibious operations will be riskier and more dispersed in the 21st century, they may still be needed.

The US Army provides the troops for such operations, but it has also studied how to do its part in a campaign which will almost certainly begin at sea and in the air. The service is focusing on improving mobility, so it can quickly move thousands of troops to crisis spots, even when those places lack existing infrastructure. This idea is known as 'places, not bases'.

The army is also skilled at handling dispersed logistics requirements since it is already present across the region. Major forces are positioned in Alaska, Hawaii, South Korea, and Japan, with added presence in Guam and Samoa. American soldiers are routinely engaged in training and exercises in Australia, the Philippines, India, Singapore, Thailand and elsewhere.

A new unit is being created which, while able to be used anywhere, seems designed for the Indo-Pacific. The Multi-Domain Task Force (MDTF) is described as a theatre-level asset, combining all the capabilities the Army can contribute to a fight which will initially require naval and air assets. The MDTF contains a long-range artillery battalion equipped with rockets, missiles and a soon-to-be-fielded hypersonic weapon. Such a battalion based in the Philippines or South Korea could strike targets around Taiwan and in mainland China. It could also strike enemy ships.

The MDTF also incorporates an air defence battalion able to augment air force and navy anti-air capabilities. A mixed battalion containing intelligence, signals, electronic warfare, and cyberwarfare companies provides added resources. The MDTF's final element is a support battalion for logistics and maintenance.

An island-hopping campaign in the Western Pacific is another possibility. A 21st-century version of this involves the seizure of undefended islands followed by the fast construction of airfields and the emplacement of air and missile defences to withstand Chinese air and missile bombardments. Such bases could control the waters around them, providing an umbrella of air cover as naval forces advance.

An exercise in late October 2022 placed army units on various islands across the Hawaiian Chain to test the concept of dispersed operations. In particular, the exercise's leaders sought to intentionally stress the logistics system to see how it performed. Over 6,000 troops took part, including company-sized elements from the Philippines, Indonesia, and Thailand.

Lt Gen Xavier Brunson, commanding I Corps in the Pacific region, stated the goal of the army's effort: "Our ability to message the things that we're doing along with our partners is great, but our will to be there is going to help us achieve our goal of no war. That's the goal: No war."

ABOVE LEFT: The Indo-Pacific hosts much of the world's shipping activity. These Special Forces soldiers train on maritime boarding, search and seizure in a South Korean port. (US ARMY, PHOTO ALTERED FOR SECURITY REASONS)

ABOVE: A reconnaissance team of the 25th Infantry Division trains with US Marines in Hawaii. The multitude of islands and littoral areas in the Pacific area demands frequent amphibious training. (US ARMY)

LEFT: Led by an Indian soldier, a squad of US infantry conduct squad tactics drills at Rajasthan, India. US and Indian troops carry out frequent training together. (US ARMY)

FUTURE WARS, FUTURE WEAPONS

Return to Europe and NATO

An old front in a new Cold War?

RIGHT: A paratrooper jumps from the back of a CH47 Chinook helicopter in Germany. The 173rd Airborne Brigade, based in Italy, provides a rapid response force for NATO. (US ARMY)

The Ukraine War alarmed many in NATO when it began in February 2022. For decades Russia had conducted smaller military operations along its borders, leading up to the seizure of Crimea in 2014. None of these attacks appeared to threaten NATO members, although the vulnerability of the Baltic states of Latvia, Lithuania and Estonia was recognised. The open and large-scale invasion of Ukraine by Russia compelled NATO to improve its own defences. The United States is deploying additional units to Europe under Operation Atlantic Resolve.

For the US Army, that means an expanded presence in NATO nations, particularly those which border Russia and Ukraine. While there is a

BELOW: The terrain in eastern Poland is open with few natural obstacles to an invader. It is a good place to station an armoured brigade. (US ARMY)

ABOVE: Once deployed to Europe soldiers must maintain their skills. This infantryman is part of a live fire exercise in Poland. (US ARMY)

ABOVE: Finnish and American soldiers fire a 120mm mortar during joint training conducted after Finland's announced intention to join NATO. (US ARMY)

ABOVE: The 101st Airborne Division maintains a brigade in Romania to bolster NATO strength. This member of the division advances during a live fire exercise. (US ARMY)

risk for the US in bringing its troops closer to Russia, previously the risk of facing invasion was wholly borne by those Russia-bordering countries. As NATO members, however, Article 5 of the NATO Charter states an armed attack against one member shall be considered an attack against them all. This means the United States, with the largest and most capable military in the alliance, would quickly become involved in any invasion of NATO territory.

While some army units are permanently stationed in Europe, the bulk of American forces present are there on a rotational basis and will likely continue to be so for the foreseeable future. Brigade Combat Teams (BCTs) rotate into a particular NATO country for a specified period, usually nine months, and are then replaced by a new brigade, often from the same division to provide continuity. Over time, this means a division can develop a body of knowledge and experience for a particular operational area.

The rotational system also allows American leadership to tailor force requirements based on the evolving threat, growing, or shrinking the troop commitment as needed. This must also be paced with the need to conduct maintenance, training, rest, and refits for units, so exhaustion does not become a concern.

For example, prior to the invasion of Ukraine the US Army posted one armoured BCT in Europe; this quickly increased to three immediately after the war began. Later in 2022, one of those BCTs rotated home without a replacement, leaving two armoured BCTs in Europe. How long two armoured BCTs will remain in theatre depends on the evolving perceived threat level.

For the immediate future it is likely the US Army commitment will stay well above pre-war levels overall, but many units will go home without being replaced; some have already done so. The Ukraine War has not gone well for Russia, and many feel the likelihood of the Russians directly attacking a NATO member is low, given their army's poor performance in Ukraine. While their nuclear weapons are always a concern, at the moment the Russians do not appear able to fight a conventional conflict on two fronts.

Small reductions in troop levels may also provide a signal to the Russians that the US does not intend to become directly involved in the Ukraine War, reducing tensions. Still, the army has left certain headquarters elements in Europe, which will facilitate the return of American BCTs if the crisis suddenly deepens. The US military has extensive capabilities and experience moving troops around the world quickly, a fact not lost on any of its potential opponents.

For now, the US Army has returned to Europe and is engaging in what is essentially a new Cold War. It will remain there for the foreseeable future, conducting a presence mission and taking part in exercises designed to increase NATO's overall readiness. Some of the tensions of the 20th century are back, but at a much lower overall threat level.

BELOW: Artillery has again proven itself the king of battle in Ukraine and every US Army brigade has a battalion of howitzers for fire support. (US ARMY)

FUTURE WARS, FUTURE WEAPONS

The Arctic

A future battleground

RIGHT: Paratroopers jump from a C-17 Globemaster in Alaska. The 11th Airborne Division is a Joint Forcible Entry unit, able to respond anywhere in the Pacific region within 18 hours. (US ARMY)

FAR RIGHT: Arctic weather conditions require frequent maintenance to keep equipment operational. This 155mm howitzer crew will spend hours cleaning and inspecting their weapon after this firing exercise. (US ARMY)

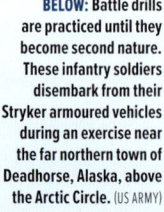

BELOW: Battle drills are practiced until they become second nature. These infantry soldiers disembark from their Stryker armoured vehicles during an exercise near the far northern town of Deadhorse, Alaska, above the Arctic Circle. (US ARMY)

In the past, the Arctic region played host to scientific expeditions, a few early warning radar stations, and the occasional submarine patrol. However, with the recession of the Arctic ice due to climate change, it is now more likely to see conflict on a large scale. As the ice melts, access to heretofore unreachable natural resources becomes possible. Oil and gas fields, mineral deposits, and precious metals such as gold are only a few of the assets becoming available.

Nations which have territory in the Arctic, including the United States, are all preparing to claim a share of these reserves. The Russians, who have vast territories above the Arctic Circle, are doing so on a large scale, forming new military units, and reactivating Cold War-era bases. Even China, which lacks lands that far north, is preparing to claim what it can for its own industrial machine.

As part of the American effort to build combat potential in the Arctic, the US Army has reactivated the 11th Airborne Division, its first new division-sized organisation in decades. The 11th is a Joint Forcible Entry unit, meaning it works with other portions of the US military to quickly strike against defended territory and hold it until reinforcement arrives, a classic airborne mission. It has also been given responsibility to develop the specialised equipment needed to function in the Arctic's harsh conditions, something the army has paid scant attention to for decades.

While this unit is earmarked for deployment anywhere in the Pacific region, it is notable that such a powerful mobile striking force is positioned in the Arctic, where it can quickly respond to a crisis or flashpoint. While the stated aim of the United States is to resolve future disputes over Arctic resources peacefully, it is expanding the ability to fight for and defend the nation's interests in a region long ignored by most of the world.

US ARMY YEARBOOK 2023

Project Convergence

Developing new methods of warfare

LEFT: Paratroopers of the 82nd Airborne Division evaluate the new Integrated Vision Augmentation System. The test will determine how well the new device interacts with other command and control systems. (US ARMY)

Weapons design has not advanced radically in the last three decades, yet they are much more lethal. This is due to the advances in digital technology and electronics, creating advanced sensors and devices which allow those weapons to be used much more quickly and accurately than ever before. New technology also enables improvements to vehicles and equipment to sustain and resupply soldiers.

Once developed, this new technology must be tested to see if it will perform as designed. The best way to do this is to put it in the hands of soldiers. They will use it under field conditions, subjecting the equipment to harsh weather, rough terrain, and simulated combat. Since soldiers are the end users of any new device, they have a vested interest in ensuring it is effective, durable, and reliable. Often, they will even devise new and unorthodox ways to employ new systems which even the designers had not considered.

For the past three years, the Project Convergence exercise has looked at how to integrate new technologies into the army and use them effectively. Project Convergence 2022 saw thousands of US Army soldiers joining with 500 British and 200 Australian troops to conduct joint tests and exercises.

"Project Convergence 22 is an all-service experiment that includes Special Operations Forces, and our UK and Australian partners. Using existing and emerging technologies from space to land and sea, PC22 will experiment with capabilities that protect against air and missile threats as well as those that will allow us to defeat anti-access defenses," said Lt Gen Scott McKean, director of this year's event.

Over 300 technologies were tested during September through November of 2022, at various locations across the western US, Hawaii, Australia, Japan, and the Philippines. The evaluated technologies included long-range long range artillery, UAVs, Autonomous vehicles, and new sensors. One experiment had the allied force form an integrated air and missile defence network and fire long range missiles at a target in the Pacific. Another test involved a Blackhawk helicopter launching drones while in flight, while the Australians launched a drone swarm, and the UK forces used several drones for a reconnaissance mission.

BOTTOM: UK soldiers from 2nd Battalion The Yorkshire Regiment employ a small drone during an exercise at Fort Irwin, California for Project Convergence. (US ARMY)

www.keymilitary.com 99

FUTURE WARS, FUTURE WEAPONS

Future Armour

A new generation of tanks and fighting vehicles

RIGHT: Rheinmetall's Lynx IFV uses a 35mm cannon and a suite of electronics enabling the crew to link and coordinate with other vehicles or units. (RHEINMETALL)

Most of the US Army's armoured vehicles are legacy models dating back to the Cold War. They have proven capable of extensive upgrades and improvements, a testament to the versatility of their design. However, new materials and technologies eventually render older vehicles obsolete, compelling the search for a replacement.

Even as the search for new designs proceeds, the army continues to upgrade its current inventory. The Advanced Targeting and Lethality Aided System (ATLAS) is under testing on the M1 Abrams. The system combines new sensor technology with machine-learning algorithms to automate tasks normally conducted by the crew during passive target acquisition. In essence, ATLAS detects targets and determines their precise location and distance, allowing the crew to engage three targets in the time it would normally take them to engage one. This is in line with the general trend toward faster target detection and attack, enabled by new technology and becoming increasingly necessary for survival on the battlefield.

A new design called Mobile Protected Firepower (MPF) is the culmination of a decades-long search for a light tank to replace the M551 Sheridan, retired in 1997. The army sought a vehicle light enough to be air-dropped, but with the firepower to engage likely threats including tanks. Several designs were extensively tested but never adopted, until the selection of the MPF vehicle.

The vehicle has not yet received an official model number or name, but a $1.14 billion contract has gone to General Dynamics Land Systems to produce 96 vehicles. Its intended use is to provide fire support to airborne and light infantry, thus the need

BELOW: This Armoured Multipurpose Vehicle is undergoing testing at the Tropic Regions Test Center in Panama. (US ARMY)

for a lightweight vehicle which is more easily transported by existing transport aircraft. The army is not calling the vehicle a tank due to its infantry support role, but elsewhere it is almost universally referred to as a light tank. The MPF weighs 38 tons and is armed with a 105mm cannon, a coaxial 7.62mm machine gun and a .50-calibre weapon atop the turret. The army currently plans to acquire about 500 MPFs and issue each infantry brigade a company with 14 vehicles.

The Armored Multi-Purpose Vehicle (AMPV) programme is a replacement for the M113 Personnel Carrier, the box-shaped, versatile vehicle which has been in service since the early 1960s. The M113 has been upgraded as far as possible, so the AMPV will be a step forward in protection, mobility and power generation, an increasingly important feature in a modern digital force. BAE Systems won the contract to produce their variant, essentially an evolution of the M2 Bradley. The AMPV is intended to operate in armoured brigades alongside the Abrams and Bradley, and their eventual replacements. Current plans call for 3,000 AMPVs in five initial variants: troop transport, command vehicle, 120mm mortar carrier and two medical vehicles.

The competition to replace the Bradley is in the design and prototype phase; most of the requirements are not publicly available. The army wants a vehicle with a 50mm cannon and the ability to move silently, with the engine off, necessitating a hybrid powertrain. Production is planned for 2030. One likely entry in the competition is Rheinmetall's Lynx, a tracked vehicle currently mounting a 35mm cannon and antitank missiles in a turret. Lynx has an armour package protecting against medium calibre guns, antitank weapons, mines and IEDs. It has an 1,100-horsepower engine able to push it up to 70kph with a range of 500km. Lynx can carry up to 11 soldiers including the crew and carries a reconnaissance drone aboard.

The army has no current plans to replace the M1 Abrams, opting to instead continue upgrading it for the time being. The service is expected to make initial decisions about an eventual replacement programme in 2023. Instead of waiting for that announcement, General Dynamics has put forth a concept vehicle called the AbramsX, an evolution of the current tank.

This new Abrams is 10 tons lighter and uses a diesel-electric engine which is 50% more fuel efficient than the current Abrams. The tank can operate in 'silent watch' mode, where the crew can operate the electronics and weapons with the engine off, reducing its thermal signature. The tank's Katalyst software, like ATLAS, will identify targets and put them in a ranked list for the crew to destroy. Its main gun is the 120mm XM360, lighter than the current weapon. Secondary weapons include a 7.62mm coaxial machine gun, a 30mm cannon mounted atop the turret in a remote-controlled station, and six Switchblade 300 loitering munitions, the famed 'kamikaze drones' used to great effect in Ukraine. The turret is unmanned, using an autoloader for the main gun. The crew of three sits in the heavily armoured hull.

ABOVE: This M1 Abrams is equipped with ATLAS, the Advanced Targeting and Lethality Aided System, which reduces the time needed to engage a target by two-thirds. (US ARMY)

ABOVE LEFT: General Dynamics announced its upgraded M1 tank in late 2022. The design uses decades of technical advancements to create a virtually new tank. (US ARMY)

BELOW: The Mobile Protected Firepower vehicle is essentially a light tank toting a 105mm cannon. Ease of transport makes it useful to light infantry brigades. (US ARMY)

FUTURE WARS, FUTURE WEAPONS

Autonomous Weapons and Vehicles

Taking humans out of harm's way

RIGHT: This Vision 60 robot is equipped as a scout and is shown being tested on a patrol route around a US base area.
(US ARMY)

This century's battlefields are much more lethal than those of World War Two or any conflict of the Cold War. Modern weapons are more accurate, deadlier, and employed more quickly, increasing the intensity of combat and its capacity for destruction and loss of life. Advances in computing and electronics are enabling ever faster cycles of target identification, allocation of forces and strikes against those targets. Digital technology is the greatest force multiplier in warfare and the next logical step is to put autonomous weapons on the battlefield.

This is a decades-old phenomenon, most apparent in the use of Unmanned Aerial Vehicles (UAVs), which are now routinely armed to carry out strikes, though usually only at the command of the human operator. Technology is on the verge of enabling truly autonomous weapons, which can locate and engage targets without any action or approval from a human being. Ethical arguments rage over whether such systems should be used.

While that debate continues, militaries worldwide are experimenting with autonomous weapons, and remotely operated vehicles. There are three categories.

'Human in the loop' systems are weapons which select and attack targets only on human command. Most armed UAVs are in this category.

'Human on the loop' weapons can select and attack targets independently but operate under the watch of a human who can override its actions.

Finally, 'human out of the loop' weapons select and attack targets with no interaction with a human.

The US Army is developing several autonomous systems, mostly vehicles. First, the Optionally Manned

BELOW: A soldier practices with the remote-control unit for an autonomous tracked carrier, before beginning a reconnaissance and resupply test run.
(US ARMY)

ABOVE: The SMET is essentially a small lorry, helping carry heavy kit that otherwise would sit on a soldier's back. (GENERAL DYNAMICS)

ABOVE: Soldiers have the option of remotely operating many of the new autonomous systems using this remote interface unit (RIU). (US ARMY)

ABOVE: The Origin is equipped for both reconnaissance and combat. Note the drone sitting on its platform at the rear of the vehicle. (US ARMY)

Fighting Vehicle (OMFV) is intended to replace the M2 Bradley Fighting Vehicle. It will be able to operate as a standard IFV with a crew or alongside its infantry complement. A notable feature is the inclusion of a hybrid powertrain to reduce fuel consumption and logistical needs.

There are also several competing designs for a small autonomous vehicle, equipped for reconnaissance but also armed with light weapons. These vehicles could accompany troops to augment their firepower and sensing capabilities. Such a vehicle could scout ahead of a body of soldiers, assuming the risk of initial enemy contact and relaying sensor data back to them. Some designs are wheeled while others use tracks. Most are around the size of a golf cart or small lorry.

One example is the Origin, a small eight-wheeled vehicle with an electronics suite for scouting, including a tethered UAV which can hover above the vehicle and improve the field of view for the soldiers it supports. Photographs of Origin showed it armed with an M240 7.62mm machine gun and a light antitank weapon. It also has limited deck space for cargo, a welcome aid to the soldiers it accompanies.

As soldier's equipment loads become ever heavier, the army is investigating robotic cargo carriers. In November 2022, General Dynamics Land Systems delivered 16 Small Multipurpose Equipment Transports (S-MET), a wheeled vehicle with a deck platform for carrying anything from extra ammunition to soldier's kit, food, or water. The vehicle can also evacuate casualties to nearby aid stations, eliminating the need to detach a pair of soldiers to carry a stretcher. S-METs might resupply units in combat, rather than risking soldiers having to carry supplies under hostile fire. They can be operated by a human using a single-hand remote controller and use a hybrid powertrain, allowing them to generate power to recharge batteries for other equipment.

General Dynamics is also developing the TRX 10-ton tracked carrier, able to carry larger payloads including weapons systems. It has applications as a weapons carrier, obstacle breacher, communications/electronic warfare vehicle or in a reconnaissance role. It also uses a hybrid powertrain.

One new design moves on legs rather than wheels or tracks. Vision 60, built by Ghost Robotics, is a quadrupedal robot already in testing with the US Air Force. It can patrol areas, using an arm attachment to investigate suspicious items and open doors. The latest version can swim, and one variant carries a ten-shot sniper rifle. For now, the sniper version is a human in the loop system.

An autonomous HIMARS rocket launcher is under evaluation with the army as well. The vehicle looks like a HIMARS launcher, but without the crew cab. It is believed the vehicle would operate alongside crewed launchers, allowing the soldiers to operate it remotely. This effectively doubles the firepower of a single HIMARS crew.

FUTURE WARS, FUTURE WEAPONS

Long-Range Artillery and Missiles

Extending the reach of the King of Battle

RIGHT: A Precision Strike Missile launches from a HIMARS rocket launcher during a test. (US SPACE FORCE)

BELOW: The XM35 155mm howitzer is a new concept for lightweight self-propelled artillery. Whether it will be produced or exists simply to test new concepts is unknown. (US ARMY)

The US Army's artillery branch saw limitations on its use during the wars in Iraq and Afghanistan, where air strikes using precision ordnance increased in the hopes of limiting collateral damage. Many artillery units deployed without their cannons or rocket launchers, instead performing infantry or security roles. An additional problem arose when, during the early 2010s, the army realised newer Russian, and Chinese artillery systems outranged current US weapons. This led to a number of new programmes designed to eliminate this shortfall.

The most ambitious was the Strategic Long Range Cannon programme, cancelled in mid-2022. This weapon would have had a range greater than 1,000 miles (1,600km), enough to allow a weapon based in South Korea to range most of eastern China or one emplaced in Latvia to hit targets in Moscow and beyond. Though the stated reasoning for the cancellation is vague, it is likely the weapon was not yet technically feasible.

Other programmes have shown more success. The Extended Range Cannon Artillery (ERCA) programme uses the existing M109 chassis, fitted with a new long barrelled 155mm gun. During testing a prototype achieved hits on target at a range of 43 miles (70km) using the Excalibur guided projectile. The weapon can also use the new XM1113 projectile, a rocket-assisted device with a range exceeding 40km. The army will equip a

104 US ARMY YEARBOOK 2023

battalion with the ECRA during 2023 and conduct a yearlong assessment under field conditions. Planned future improvements include an autoloader to increase the rate of fire and a new fuse which increases accuracy nearly to the standard of GPS guidance.

Dark Eagle is the army's long range hypersonic weapons system. While the actual missiles themselves have not yet been announced as in service, a battery of the 3rd Artillery Regiment has been equipped with the launcher and firing apparatus. The unit is training with the equipment and developing procedures so that when the missiles become available, they can quickly transition to an operational status and train additional firing batteries as they are stood up.

The Precision Strike Missile (PrSM) is the replacement for the ATACMS missile, in service since the 1980s. Initially, maximum range was 499km due to treaty restrictions with Russia, but the US withdrew from that treaty in 2019, stating Russia had already broken it. The weapon is now in initial production and should enter service in 2023. Range has been improved to beyond 500km, but its maximum range is classified. The PrSM is designed for use in the army's existing MLRS and HIMARS launchers, with two missiles in each ammunition pod rather than a single ATACMS, doubling each launcher's firepower.

A fourth system, named simply Mid-Range Capability (MRC), seeks to cover the gap between the PrSM and the eventual hypersonic weapon. It is also planned to enter service in late 2023 using the existing Tomahawk cruise missile and the SM6 Standard missile, both navy weapons adapted for new use by the Army. These weapons have an antiship capability, which the army has not had since the now defunct World War Two-era Coast Artillery. Such a capability could prove useful in the Pacific and elsewhere; MRC batteries emplaced on islands could strike enemy warships or land targets, increasing the threat facing an opponent.

These weapons would be incorporated into the Army's proposed Multi-Domain Task Forces (MDTF). These units combine artillery, air defence, and intelligence units into a theatre-level asset. The artillery would exist within a Strategic Fires Battalion, equipped with three batteries, equipped with PrSM-equipped HIMARS, MRC and Long-Range Hypersonic weapons, respectively. Such a battalion would provide a new long-range capability for the artillery, allowing strikes without having to risk aircraft against adversaries with advanced air defence networks.

Finally, a new lightweight 155mm self-propelled weapon is under development. The XM35 is a tracked vehicle which can be transported by air. The work is being conducted by the Rock Island Arsenal in Illinois, the army's traditional artillery production centre and actually located on an island in the Mississippi River on the border between Iowa and Illinois. There are no announcements as to adoption or full-scale production, however.

ABOVE: Once operational, Dark Eagle will place hypersonic weapons into army use for the first time. (US ARMY)

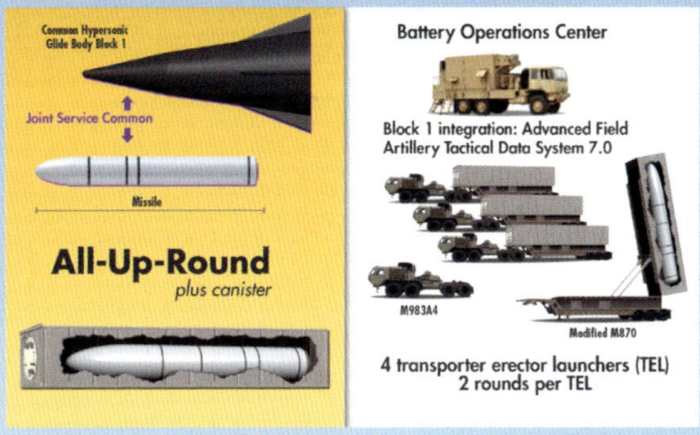

ABOVE: Dark Eagle batteries will contain four launchers with two missiles each, plus a Fire Direction Centre (FDC) and trucks carrying extra missiles to reload the launchers. (US ARMY)

BELOW: The Extended Range Cannon Artillery system provides US artillery units with longer range to compete with newer foreign designs. (US ARMY)

FUTURE WARS, FUTURE WEAPONS

New Aviation Systems

Replacing legacy designs

RIGHT: The V280's cockpit displays give pilots better situational awareness and the flight systems are upgradeable, to include eventual remote piloting.
(US ARMY)

BELOW: Concept art of Sikorsky's Raider X attack/reconnaissance helicopter escorting cargo helicopters over a Pacific jungle.
(LOCKHEED MARTIN)

Like its armoured vehicles, almost all the Army's helicopters are legacy designs, dating back to 1962 in the case of the CH47 Chinook and 1979 for the UH60 Blackhawk. The AH64 Apache is a relative newcomer, dating to 1986. All these models are older than most of their pilots. All of them have been upgraded several times during their service, but new designs taking advantage of progress in technology and materials are on the horizon.

The Army is taking part in the US military's Future Vertical Lift programme, meant to devise a new family of helicopters, sharing as many components as possible and replacing all the Army's current aircraft. Several major defence companies are developing entries for the competition, and aggressively promoting their own concepts.

One award has been made for the army's Future Long Range Assault Aircraft (FLRAA), its cargo and transport helicopter. The Bell V280 Valor is a tiltrotor design, similar to the V22 Osprey. The army wants an aircraft which can fly up to 2,800 miles (4,506km) without refuelling, though the Valor is still reportedly a few hundred miles short of that target. The prototype has shown other capabilities, such as a 350mph (563kph) cruising speed, low speed manoeuvrability and long-range cruising ability. Production aircraft will carry up to 14 troops and a crew of four.

Bell used feedback from army pilots, mechanics and even infantry squads during the V280's design phase. It is set to replace about 2,000 Blackhawks currently in service. This is the largest helicopter purchase in the army's history and could be worth up to $70 billion over time.

The AH64 Apache will be replaced by the Future Attack Reconnaissance Aircraft (FARA). The Army has stated FARA is the number one modernisation priority for its aviation branch and the third most important modernisation effort overall. The army was employing the AH64 as its attack helicopter and the OH58 Kiowa as its scout helicopter. With the retirement of the Kiowa, the AH64 has been performing both roles, assisted by Shadow drones.

In March 2020, two finalists were chosen to develop prototypes, but in May 2022, flight testing was delayed until Fiscal Year 2024 due to budget issues. The selectees, Bell and Sikorsky, will compete for final selection. Bell is a subsidiary of Textron Corporation while Sikorsky falls under Lockheed Martin.

The Bell entry, the 360 Invictus, is a single rotor design with a tandem cockpit and retractable weapons racks. The landing gear also retracts, allowing for increased airspeed and lowering the aircraft's radar signature. A pair of stub wings increases lift and reduces stress on the rotors. It is armed with a 20mm cannon in a chin turret, like the Apache. The weapons racks can carry a variety of rockets and missiles. The Invictus also uses a supplemental power unit to increase cruising speed and for ground maintenance checks.

LEFT: An infantry squad from the 101st Airborne Division went to the Bell factory to test the V-280's cabin configuration. (US ARMY)

Sikorsky's design, the Raider X, is an evolution of the S-97 Raider, developed for a cancelled Aerial Scout helicopter programme. The aircraft uses a coaxial rotor system (two rotors, one over the other) and a pusher prop at the rear for increased manoeuvrability. It also features a cannon in a chin turret and retractable weapons racks and landing gear.

Both the Bell and Sikorsky designs will incorporate modern fly by wire control systems and advanced electronics and sensors. This technology enables them to communicate with various friendly elements such as other aircraft, ground units and headquarters, as well as having better target detection and engagement capabilities.

LEFT: The Bell 360 attack/reconnaissance helicopter's stub wings sit over the retractable weapons racks and provide extra lift for the aircraft. (BELL)

BELOW: A V-280 Valor performing a flight demonstration in 2020. The prototype flew over 214 hours and demonstrated a high cruising speed. (US ARMY)

FUTURE WARS, FUTURE WEAPONS

Air Defence

Countering a widening range of threats

MAIN: It is still unclear whether more purchases are forthcoming, but the army has extensively tested the Israeli Iron Dome system, as seen here at a New Mexico test range.
(US ARMY)

TOP RIGHT: The US uses NASAMS to defend Washington DC and the system is now seeing combat use in Ukraine.
(KONGSBERG DEFENCE AND AEROSPACE)

BOTTOM RIGHT: GhostEye is a new radar for medium range anti-aircraft systems. It can detect, identify, and track cruise missiles, drones, aircraft, and helicopters.
(RAYTHEON MISSILES AND DEFENSE)

Though no major purchases are announced for the near future, development continues on several air defence systems. Versatility is the key to future air defences, as new weapons must be able to intercept a wide array of targets. These include not only fixed-wing aircraft and helicopters, but also drones, cruise missiles, ballistic missiles, and even hypersonic weapons in the near future.

Sometimes increased capability does not require brand new weapons. Raytheon is developing GhostEye, an advanced radar which can be paired with new or existing missile systems, such as the MIM104 Patriot. While the army is seeking a replacement for the effective but decades-old Patriot, it is still in the testing phase. The new system, called Integrated Air and Missile Defense Battle Command System, or IBCS, has downed several targets during limited testing.

The army purchased several of the Israeli Iron Dome systems and has been evaluating them without further purchase thus far. American defence company Raytheon has partnered with Israeli manufacturer Rafael to build and market the Iron Dome. It is unclear whether the system will see wider US usage.

The Multi-Mission Launcher (MML) has been under extended development for at least six years, partially because it is a testbed system. Mounting 15 launch tubes on a standard army truck, Sidewinder, Hellfire, Stinger, and Israeli Tamir missiles have all been investigated. A small missile called Miniature Hit To Kill (M-HTK) was also assessed; it lacks a warhead and depends upon physically striking the target. There are also plans to integrate a laser weapon.

The National Advanced Surface to Air Missile System (NASAMS) is peculiar in that it has only been purchased by the US to protect the Washington DC area. It is produced by Raytheon in partnership with Norwegian company Kongsberg. In mid-2022 several NASAMS were transferred to Ukraine to be used against Russian missiles and aircraft.

US ARMY YEARBOOK 2023

The Future Soldier's Equipment

Enabling the individual soldier to fight and survive

ABOVE: Under development and testing for a decade, the Nett Warrior End User Device uses a Samsung Note Smart Phone to provide navigation, situational awareness and information sharing among small units. (US ARMY)

LEFT: The new Modular Scalable Vest is lighter than previous body armour and comes in a wider range of sizes to better fit female soldiers. (US ARMY)

ABOVE: The Secure Handhelds on Assured Resilient networks at the tactical Edge (SHARE) is a communication device for sharing data securely in the field. Compared to current systems it is extremely compact for ease of transportation. (US ARMY)

LEFT: Small drones such as this InstantEye are proliferating through the army; soldiers can take advantage of its camera or infrared illuminator. (US ARMY)

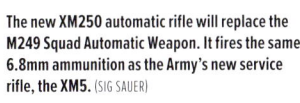

The new XM250 automatic rifle will replace the M249 Squad Automatic Weapon. It fires the same 6.8mm ammunition as the Army's new service rifle, the XM5. (SIG SAUER)

FUTURE WARS, FUTURE WEAPONS

New UAVs and How to Fight Them

Using them and bringing them down

Unmanned Aerial Vehicles (UAVs), already widely used, will only become more prevalent in future combat. The US military began using drones in the 1960s for Intelligence, Surveillance and Reconnaissance (ISR) missions over communist China and Vietnam. The 1991 Gulf War saw more use of UAVs and over time they became larger, more capable and started carrying weapons. In the 21st century armed and unarmed drones are standard tools in any advanced military; with the advent of 'kamikaze drones', sometimes the UAV is the weapon.

Two recent UAV developments are making modern battlefields yet more dangerous, as evidenced by their use in Ukraine. Loitering munitions are UAVs which fly to a likely enemy-occupied area, 'loiter' (i.e., look for a suitable target) and then attack it, destroying the UAV in the process. These are also called kamikaze drones.

As UAVs become cheaper and easier to manufacture, drone swarms are also proliferating. Drones are not terribly difficult to knock out of the sky, but if there are 50 or 100 of them attacking even a brigade-sized unit, its anti-drone assets can be quickly saturated and overwhelmed. Army units rotating through exercises at the National Training Center in California routinely face drone swarms to help them learn how to engage and defeat them. As drones become less expensive, drone swarms are easier to create and use; the Army is also experimenting with low-cost 3D printed drones.

The US Switchblade drone is an example of a loitering munition, but improved designs are on the way. BAE Systems' Concept 1 UAV carries a 40kg payload, has four hours of endurance and can cruise at .5 Mach at 30,000 feet altitude. If not expended, it can be recovered and used later. With its capabilities and expected cost it would not likely be used against a single tank, for

RIGHT: The Textron Aerosonde MK4.7 is another ISR platform undergoing testing by the army. It can land by flying into a net from which it can be quickly recovered.
(US ARMY)

RIGHT: Drone Buster is another electronic weapon for disabling UAVs. It is compact, lightweight, and quick to employ, useful against small drones which can appear quickly overhead.
(US ARMY)

LEFT: A relocatable unattended ground sensor is assessed during Project Convergence 2022. It is used for ISR and is fully autonomous, even able to recharge automatically (US ARMY)

LEFT: This drone carries a magnetometer for detecting underground munitions. In field use this could make mine clearance safer. (US ARMY CORPS OF ENGINEERS)

example, but might strike a command post or logistics node.

Designed as a possible replacement for the Army's MQ1C Grey Eagle, the General Atomics' Mojave has 25 hours endurance and can be ready to fly 1.5 hours after being delivered by a C130 cargo plane. Powered by a Rolls Royce M250 engine, Mojave can carry up to 16 Hellfire missiles along with its integral sensors. During testing, it has taken off and landed in less than 500 feet (152m). The manufacturer claims Mojave is meant for surveillance, close air support and armed overwatch of ground troops.

Soldiers are also gaining new ways of defending against UAV attacks. Many current anti-aircraft weapons are effective against various types of drones, but with small, cheap designs now common, it makes little sense to destroy a £300 drone with a £120,000 missile. Luckily cheaper but effective options exist. Rifle-sized electronic weapons such the Drone Defender use radio frequency blockers to jam a drone's signal. Another device, Drone Buster, performs a similar function in a smaller handheld device. Some variants can even block GPS signals.

Laser weapons are proving effective against drones at a very low cost. Current laser weapons are power hungry and must be mounted on vehicles (see page 24). However, those weapons are becoming more powerful and eventually will get smaller, enabling them to be issued to troops other than air defence specialists. Machine guns started as a specialist's weapon, but now every field unit has them. The same is becoming the norm for anti-UAV weapons.

FUTURE WARS, FUTURE WEAPONS

The future of the US Army

Challenges, new and old, but opportunities as well

The US Army is in a period of transition. For two decades the military was focused largely on the War on Terror, which drained much of its focus away from preparing for conflicts with potential adversaries who pose much greater, even existential, threats to the United States. The two greatest of these possible enemies, China and Russia, have not wasted the opportunity to develop new weapons and try to improve their armies.

However, America has been in this situation before. After the Vietnam conflict, the US Army was a depleted force, with dissension in the ranks, military service unpopular with the citizenry, and facing a much-

RIGHT: US Secretary of Defense Lloyd Austin meets with Ukrainian President Volodymyr Zelensky. Training and equipping Ukrainian forces are a continuing priority for the US Army. (US DoD)

BELOW: Training with NATO allies is a top priority. An M1 tank crosses the Nestos River in Greece. (US ARMY)

US ARMY YEARBOOK 2023

LEFT: Combining night and thermal vision provides a clearer image for soldiers operating in darkness. (US ARMY)

improved Soviet Army with new weaponry. Recognising its problems, the US Army rebuilt; today there are no major problems in the ranks and soldiers are held in high regard in American society. The Army also created many of the weapons it still uses today: the M1 Abrams tank, Bradley Fighting Vehicle, M270 MLRS and the AH64 Apache, to name a few.

In the 21st century it faces a growing Chinese threat, and a Russia which, while bogged down in Ukraine, shows no signs of quitting that conflict soon. Russia has also developed a range of new weapons, though whether it can afford to buy or build them is an open debate. Iran and North Korea continue to be lesser threats which could still pose problems in various ways.

The Ukraine war continues to demand the US Army's attention due to its role in training and equipping the Ukrainian forces. Even when the war ends, the need to rebuild Ukraine's army will draw resources. While this draws money and focus away from the Army's other priorities, the effort is manageable for the time being. Despite the cost, depleting Russia's military so it cannot effectively operate elsewhere lowers the risk of direct conflict with them. The Ukrainians are spending by spilling blood for their nation; the US need only spend money.

Efforts to upgrade existing weapons and equipment will continue. As stated, many of its legacy weapon systems have been in service for four to five decades. While it is finally replacing some of those systems, others will continue to see use, perhaps for decades, albeit in upgraded form. In some cases, this is due to the expense of replacing them; in others, there simply isn't any new technology superior enough to justify that replacement.

New weapons are also entering service, and this will continue throughout the decade. Drones, while not a new weapon, will see far wider use with better capabilities. Autonomous weapons are on the cusp of practical use, as are energy weapons. New artillery weapons such as extended range cannons, the Precision Strike Missile and the Dark Eagle hypersonic weapon will enable the Army to strike from a distance. New long-range helicopters and vehicles with hybrid powertrains will support this new ability to operate over wider swaths of territory.

Some challenges remain, however. Arming the Ukrainians has drained some US stockpiles and the lessons learned from that conflict will likely point out weaknesses to be redressed. Some of the new weapon programmes are experiencing difficulties for which the solutions may prove expensive or simply unsolvable with present technology. US military budgets have climbed drastically over the past two decades and it remains to be seen whether the money will continue to be there for what the service believes it needs.

Weapons and equipment are just a part of the solution. The US Army will seek to maintain its relationships with existing partners and allies, expand them where possible and even develop new ones in line with US policies. Training exercises and joint operations are key to forming effective fighting coalitions in case of war; they will be frequent and build upon one another over time. The US Army knows allies are the key to success for a force with worldwide commitments.

The Army's best asset will remain its soldiers. Without well-trained and disciplined troops, no new weapon or tactic will likely succeed. In the 2020s, the US Army's pool of experienced soldiers and leaders, battle hardened yet understanding that the wars of tomorrow will be different from what they faced in the past, are the key to victory.

BELOW: Long range artillery rocket and missile systems are a top priority for development in the 2020s. (US ARMY)

GLOSSARY

US Army Yearbook Glossary

The A to X of the US Army

A2/AD: Anti-Access/Area Denial
ABCT: Armoured Brigade Combat Team
ACE: Armoured Combat Earthmover
ACR: Armoured Cavalry Regiment
AFRICOM: Africa Command
AH: Attack Helicopter
AIT: Advanced Individual Training
AMPV: Armoured Multi-Purpose Vehicle
ARNG: Army National Guard
ATACMS: – Army Tactical Missile System
ATLAS: Advanced Targeting and Lethality Aided System
BCT: Brigade Combat Team or Basic Combat Training
BN: Battalion
CAB: Combat Aviation Brigade
CBRN: Chemical, Biological, Radiological and Nuclear
CONUS: Continental United States
EARF: East Africa Response Force
ECT: Expeditionary Cyber and electromagnetic activities Team
ERCA: Extended Range Cannon Artillery
EUCOM: European Command
EW: Electronic Warfare
EWPMT: Electronic Warfare Planning and Management Tool
FAB: Field Artillery Brigade
FARA: Future Attack Reconnaissance Aircraft

FLRAA: Future Long Range Assault Aircraft
GPS: Global Positioning System
HEMTT: Heavy Expanded Mobility Tactical Truck
HIMARS: High Mobility Artillery Rocket System
HMMWV: High Mobility Multipurpose Wheeled Vehicle
IBCT: Infantry Brigade Combat Team
IED: Improvised Explosive Device
IFV: Infantry Fighting Vehicle
INSCOM: Intelligence and Security Command
IRF: Immediate Response Force
IS: the so-called Islamic State, also known as ISIS or Da'esh
ISR: Intelligence, Surveillance and Reconnaissance
IVAS: Integrated Visual Augmentation System
JMTG-U: Joint Multinational Training Group – Ukraine
LPVO: Low-Powered Variable Optic
MDTF: Multi-Domain Task Force
MGS: Mobile Gun System
M-HTK: Miniature Hit To Kill
MLRS: Multiple Launch Rocket System
MML: Multi-Mission Launcher
MP: Military Police
MPF: Mobile Protected Firepower
MRAP: Mine Resistant, Ambush Protected
MRC: Mid-Range Capability
M-SHORAD: Manoeuvre Short-Range Air Defence

NASAMS: National Advanced Surface to Air Missile System
NATO: North Atlantic Treaty Organisation
NCO: Non-Commissioned Officer
NVA: North Vietnamese Army
OCS: Officer Candidate School
OCP: Operational Camouflage Pattern
OMFV: Optionally Manned Fighting Vehicle
OPFOR: Opposing or Opposition Force
PrSM: Precision Strike Missile
RAP: Rocket Assisted Projectile
ROTC: Reserve Officer's Training Corps
RPG: Rocket Propelled Grenade
SAW: Squad Automatic Weapon
SINCGARS: Single Channel Ground and Airborne Radio System
S-MET: Small Multipurpose Equipment Transport
SOAR: Special Operations Aviation Regiment
SOCOM: Special Operations Command
STT: Satellite Transportable Terminal
TF: Task Force
THAAD: Terminal High Altitude Area Défense
UAS: Unmanned Aerial System
UAV: Unmanned Aerial Vehicle
UH: Utility Helicopter
USARJ: United States Army Japan
USARPAC: US Army, Pacific
USFK: United States Forces Korea
XM: Experimental Model

PHOTO CREDITS:

Christopher Miskimon, US Army, US Army Reserve, US DoD, Hawaii NG, Idaho NG, Indiana NG, Maryland NG, Minnesota NG, New Jersey NG, North Carolina NG, Pennsylvania NG, Rhode Island NG, Tennessee NG, Texas NG, Washington NG, US Navy, US Marine Corps, US National Archives, US Air Force, US Missile Defense Agency, US Space Force, US Army Corps of Engineers, SIG Sauer Inc., Oshkosh Defence, Rheinmetall, General Dynamics, Bell, Lockheed Martin, Raytheon Missiles and Defense, Kongsberg Defence and Aerospace, General Atomics .

* The author has attempted, where possible, to credit the originators of all the images used in this publication. Any errors will be corrected in future editions.

BELOW: A time delay image of an M2 Bradley in the desert at Fort Irwin, California. (US ARMY)